W9-BDK-683

Everest
Diary

Books by John D. McCallum

Everest Diary
Six Roads from Abilene
That Kelly Family
The Tiger Wore Spikes
Dumb Dan
This Was Football
Scooper
and others

Everest
Diary

Based on the personal diary of *Lute Jerstad*
one of the first five Americans to conquer
Mount Everest

by John D. McCallum

FOLLETT
PUBLISHING
COMPANY

Chicago

New York

Designed by Patrick J. Birch

Follett Publishing Company
1000 West Washington Boulevard
T/L 2330   Chicago, Illinois 60607

Foreword

by James Ramsey Ullman

Nothing in my life has given me more satisfaction than my role as rear-echelon team member and "official historian" of the American Mount Everest Expedition of 1963. Now, as a bonus, I am given the added pleasure of introducing this other record of that great adventure.

In contrast to my own book, *Americans on Everest*, there is nothing at all "official" about *Everest Diary*. And that is all to the good, for two stories on the same subject, written from the same point of view, would surely trip over each other. There is, however, no tripping here. For, whereas *Americans on Everest* was, of its basic nature, a general and overall record, these memoirs of one of our country's outstanding mountaineers are as intimate and personal as a record well can be.

With Lute Jerstad, in the pages that follow, we do not merely climb Everest—we *live* Everest. We live with, and within, a man whose experience was not only of the flesh but of the mind and spirit. The ice and the snow are there all right; the heights and the depths, the wind and the cold. And these we share with him. But we share, also, his hopes and fears, his strengths and weaknesses, his joys and miseries. We watch his struggle to sleep, to eat, to keep going. We hear him playing his ukulele, singing his songs, cursing his ailments, cheering his companions, and on the frozen heights offering his humble prayer, "Please, God, watch over us." At last, on his day of days, we follow him, step by step, as he becomes one of the first twelve men ever to have stood on the summit of the earth. And that same night, with him and his three teammates, we survive an ordeal of body and spirit such as few men have ever been called upon to endure.

That this is a story of skill and endurance, courage and resolution, goes without saying. But it is also a story that is intensely, movingly human. Much of it is told in Lute's own words, exactly as he set them down in his battered notebook during his weeks on the mountain. The rest has been deftly put together from Lute's telling by writer John D. McCallum. And from the collaboration, I think, emerges a picture of the expedition as it truly was: a blend of outward and inward, of action and the meaning of action, of common cause and deep personal commitment. In short, a story not only of what men have *done*, but of what they *are*.

Enough prologue. What Lute Jerstad and his fellow Everesters did and are will become amply apparent in the pages that follow, and there is no need for me to gild the lily, other than to say that I am proud and happy to write this introduction to this book.

Contents

Everest Diary

*Though as Americans we take special pride
that our countrymen have gone to the far
horizon of experience . . . this is an international
effort in which man pits himself against his
friend and enemy — nature.*

President John F. Kennedy
July 8, 1963

1

The Time, the Place, the Men

The last wisps of dawn fog were dissolving, and though the sun had not yet risen, the valley walls were drawing color from the brightening sky. Higher up, the snow fields gleamed with a delicate pink flame in the light from beyond the horizon. After days of miserable weather, clear skies heartened the climbers.

Lute Jerstad looked up past the tapering summits of the Himalayas toward the world of rock, ice, and fierce wind that was going to be his home for the next few months. They had been traveling steadily for two and a half weeks, making good time, but the worst was yet to come. Beyond Namche Bazar the pace would slacken woefully, and Lute guessed it would be at least another two weeks before they reached the site of Base Camp, at 17,800 feet, and had their tents set up and stocked. Making the advance march of some 180 miles from Katmandu to Base Camp were 18 Americans, a British liaison officer, 37 Sherpa specialists, and 908 coolie porters. Only the Americans and Sherpas would stay at Base Camp, however—the official body of the 1963 American Everest Expedition.

The night of March 6 had been spent just outside the tiny village of Ghat, and now they were moving on up to Namche Bazar, a journey of about 10 miles. In single file they walked, a column of heavy loads, hunched backs, and bobbing heads reaching nearly 4 miles from end to end. When the caravan broke camp that morning and hit the trail, Lute joined Barry Bishop, Will Siri, and Dick Pownall up at the front.

Lute trudged along in silence, his back bent forward under his 35-pound load, his stubby legs moving like quick, steady pendulums. Without stopping, he hitched his muscular shoulders slightly and shifted the weight of his pack. It was a fairly heavy load, but he had been carrying it for almost two hours without resting, and he knew now that any doubts he may have had about his legs not being in condition could be dismissed. He had been fighting off a chest cold for the last several days, but it was subsiding now and his breathing was growing stronger. With satisfaction he felt the bite of the broad pack straps against his shoulders and the supple play of his muscles answering their pressure. He felt the strong, even thrust of his thighs and knees and the steady tramp of his boots on the trail. Yes, except for his cold, he was in excellent shape. He was prepared for any punishing eventuality.

As he hiked along the trail, Lute's mind was occupied with the curious fact that the United States, pioneer in so many explorations, had no history involving Everest. Although the mighty mountain had stirred the imaginations of men for more than a hundred years, no all-American team of climbers ever had participated in previous failures or successes.

The story of Everest began in 1852, when a clerk in the office of the Indian Trigonometrical Survey glanced up from a page of figures one day and casually told his superior: "Sir, I have just discovered the highest mountain on earth." His calculations proved him correct. The remote Himalayan summit, then listed on the charts only as "Peak XV," was estimated to be approximately 29,000 feet high, give or take a few feet; a recent computation has established the true height at 29,028 feet—many hundreds of feet taller than its closest rival. Later the gigantic peak was named for Sir George Everest, the first Surveyor-General of India. What began as a prosaic exercise in higher mathematics was eventually to become one of the great adventures of modern man.

For half a century after its discovery, Everest remained a mountain of mystery, and for another 51 years it remained unclimbed and unopposed, until Sir Edmund Hillary of Great Britain finally stood on its crest with Sherpa Tenzing Norkay, on May 29, 1953. Up to that day, ten expeditions and hundreds of competent mountaineers had failed. Fifteen had given their lives. Yet, until now, no American expedition had ever set foot on the slopes of Everest, and a question that had for many years entered the minds of Alpine clubs all around the world was whether Americans were capable of conquering its summit.

Lute picked his way mechanically over the broken ground. The world they were entering was one of stillness and desolation. There was the gray rock, the white snow, the blue sky—and that was all there was. Pausing occasionally, Lute stared at the Himalayas around him, towering gray and monstrous and forbidding. They were nearing an elevation of about 12,000 feet now, and he thought *It's like passing from one world into an entirely new one.* It wasn't so many years ago that the Sherpas, somewhat more superstitious than they are today, believed that up there somewhere, near the top of Everest, strange demon gods lurked, ready to destroy anyone who would dare venture onto its sacred slopes. With the British expedition in 1953, Tenzing Norkay had been asked what he thought their chances were of putting men on the summit, and the famous Sherpa's eyes clouded briefly. "I think we wait and see," he said solemnly. "Bad luck talk too much beforehand. With mountains, there are superstitions. . . ."

Lute trudged on, up at the head of the column. The only sound between earth and sky was the creaking of the climbers' pack straps and the dry rasp of rock beneath their boots. After 16 days, the route from Katmandu to Namche Bazar had yet to afford them their first glimpse of Everest. It had been wholly obscured by clouds during the early stages of the march, but they knew it was there, waiting— waiting to meet their challenge.

The sun was high up in its arc now, and Lute could see for miles. Far below him he could see the pastures and the forests, the paths and the streams of the lower valleys; but best of all he loved what he saw above him—the still, empty world above the tree line.

It was midafternoon and they were approaching the top of a hill overlooking Namche Bazar when they saw it. . . .

Barry Bishop was the first. He had been slightly ahead of the others, traveling at a fairly brisk pace. Suddenly he came to the top of the hill where he could look out at the horizon. He neither pointed nor cried out, but his companions knew instantly what it was. Swiftly—silently—they came up one by one and stood alongside Barry and raised their eyes with his.

Everest!

It stood like a monument: great, terrible, and alone. It rose cliff upon cliff, ridge upon ridge, tower upon tower, until the sharp, curving wedge of its summit seemed to pierce the very heart of the sky. It was a pyramid built up of a thousand parts—out of granite and limestone and snow and ice, out of glaciers, precipices, crags, ledges, spires, and cornices. Beside Everest, the other great Himalaya giants escaped notice. Such was its unchallenged and isolated supremacy.

Lute felt the catch of his breath and the wild surging of his heart. He had spent years reading, dreaming, planning for this moment, but now that it was here statistics and geology, knowledge, thought and plans were as remote and forgotten as the faraway Western cities from which he and his fellow Americans had come. He was a man bereft of everything but eyes, everything but the single electric perception: *There it is!* It seemed, somehow, less to tower than to crouch—a white-hooded giant, secret and remote, an antagonist, breathing and on guard.

Barry Bishop stood a little in front of the others. He was absolutely motionless, his face tense and serious, his eyes devouring the last thousand feet of

Everest. Lute could sense in Barry the bursting desire to act, to come to grips, to conquer. Slightly behind him stood Will Siri and Dick Pownall: they were still, their eyes cast upward.

For a long while no one spoke or moved. The only sounds between earth and sky were the soft hiss of their breathing and the pounding of their hearts. The mood of that moment was later captured in Lute's diary:

There it stands. Everest. Its pyramid thrusts savagely into the blue sky like a great white monster. Its gigantic plume of snow at the summit, buffeted by fierce winds, presents an incredible sight. Now that we are here we are asking ourselves if we really can go all the way to the top. We especially question our chances of putting a team up from the West Ridge side. Suddenly we feel very humble and insignificant —suddenly we wonder if we should even be here at all. . . .

Through the next couple of hours they wound slowly between the great ridges with their heavy loads, and at sundown they pitched camp on the outskirts of Namche Bazar. After dinner, as was their custom, the Americans sat about the camp discussing the events of the day and plans for the next.

The conversation droned on, veering from the weather, to the porters, to the Sherpas, routes, camps and strategy—the inevitable, inexhaustible topics of the climber's world.

There were all kinds of men among the 18 Americans, men with a great diversity of background and interest. They included the leader of the expedition, Norman Dyhrenfurth, a naturalized U.S. citizen from Switzerland who had accompanied a Swiss Everest assault in 1952; Dr. Will Siri, professor of physiology at University of California, and deputy leader of the expedition; Barry Bishop, a member of the foreign editorial staff of the National Geographic Society; Jake Breitenbach, a professional mountain guide who ran a climbing-skiing store at Jackson, Wyoming; Barry Corbet, operator of the Alp Horn Lodge at Jackson; Dr. Dave Dingman, a former Dartmouth hockey star who now practiced medicine in Baltimore; Al Auten, a Denver ski patrolman and editor of an engineering publication; Dan Doody, a Hollywood motion-picture cameraman; Dr. Dick Emerson, professor of sociology at the University of Cincinnati; Dr. Tom Hornbein, an M.D. from San Diego; Willi Unsoeld, former professor of theology at Oregon State University; Dr. James Lester, who was in charge of the psychological phase of the expedition's research program; Dr. Maynard Miller, a native of Tacoma, Washington, now a noted glaciologist at Michigan State University; Dick Pownall, a schoolteacher in Denver; Barry Prather, from Ellensburg, Washington; Dr. Gil Roberts, chief medical officer; Jim Whittaker, tallest man on the team at 6 feet 5 inches, a veteran mountaineer from Redmond, Washington; and, of course, Lute himself.

Certainly they were one of the most literate groups ever assembled for an assault on nature. Among them were five Ph.D. degrees, two candidates for the Ph.D. degree, and five with Master's degrees.

A man with big dreams needs a big team, and the men Norman Dyhrenfurth chose to accompany him were a combination of brain and extraordinary brawn. He ferreted out the finest collection of mountaineering minds he could find in America; dependable men of science; men with the ability to live together in tents at close quarters for weeks at a time; men who could bear up under severe strain, stress, and psychological pressures, men of extensive education. All of the men present had met Norman's requirements: They were college men; experienced climbers; willing to quit their jobs or get a leave of absence and sign on with the expedition at no pay; and they had agreed to put up a deposit of $500 apiece in cash, to be refunded when the expedition returned. They were willing to be human guinea pigs for the many physical and psychological tests that the scientists and doctors would conduct.

Granted, the requirements were stiff, but it was Norman's theory that any man who was willing to meet such standards was the sort of dedicated man he wanted on his side when the going grew tough. For this was going to be more than solely a mountaineering venture. It was also going to be highly scientific in nature. They would be making studies in glaciology, weather, and solar radiation. They would measure how mind and body react to fatigue, isolation, cold, sleeplessness, and dehydration at high altitudes. In other words, the winning of Everest was not to be a stunt to be admired, briefly cheered, and then pushed aside into the obscurity of history. Like the exploration of space, of the poles, of the depths of the seas, it was going to be part of the continuing process of man's expansion of his frontiers.

For 44-year-old Norman Dyhrenfurth this was the culmination of years of planning, working, and waiting. He had not only conceived the idea of leading the first all-American expedition to Everest, but he had also personally selected the men, raised more than $400,000 to finance the project, enlisted the aid of private corporations to equip it, won the official support of government and scientific leaders in the United States, and negotiated the agreement with the Nepalese government for permission to climb Everest. It had been a very tall order, because there had been numerous political barriers to hurdle before the Americans could even make their attempt. The high Himalayas were no longer merely the frontier between Central and Southern Asia; they were also the frontier between the Communist countries and the Free World. Tibet had long ago withdrawn behind the Bamboo Curtain, and its access to Everest was closed to the Americans. The only way to Everest for the Americans was through Nepal, and Norman had to wait nearly three years before he acquired formal permission to lead the expedition past Nepalese border ranges.

Such were the men who huddled in down clothing in the deep, still cold of a Himalayan night. There were, to be sure, many differences among them, in temperament as well as in background. But differences were unimportant. What mattered—all that mattered—was that their purpose was one: to carry out their scientific research successfully and to climb the heights of rock and ice looming above them in the night; to stand for a moment where no American had ever stood before. To that end they had come from half a world away, across oceans and continents to the remoteness of inner Asia. To that end they were prepared to endure frightening cold, exhaustion, and danger—even death. Why? There is no real answer, and at the same time every man among them knew the answer: *He had to meet the challenge of his inner self.*

The night grew cold and damp, and Lute, still tired from his chest cold, swallowed an antibiotic and crawled into his sleeping bag. Tiredness outweighed his discomfort, and he soon dropped off to sleep. While he slept, he dreamed of rock and ice and the vastness below and above. Everest pervaded even the world of sleep.

When he awoke, it was almost dawn. It had grown bitterly cold during the night, and his joints were stiff and his fingers and toes almost numb. The air was clear and the sky was still dark, but the stars had disappeared and the mountain walls above were swathed in drifting mist. The dream Lute had had during the night was still with him, and in his mind's eye he could picture Everest rising out of the great white range of mountains, immense and alone, a single, unforgettable shape. He knew it was no illusion, no trick of the imagination, because only yesterday he had seen the last thousand feet of the massive peak with his own eyes. It was a fact. It existed, and though he couldn't see it from where he stood now, he knew it hovered far above him—vast, still, and immutable.

2

The Preliminaries

Much of what the Americans knew about their chances of surviving on Everest—and what to expect in the way of physical and psychological harassment —had been learned six months before on Mount Rainier in the state of Washington. Rainier, volcanic in origin, is king of the Cascades, a range of mountains with near-Himalayan conditions extending for some 500 miles through Washington and Oregon. Rainier is a magnificent snow dome whose 14,410 feet make it the fifth highest mountain in the continental United States. This dormant volcano is famous not only for climbing, but as an all-year ski playground, its summit ice cap and its encircling glaciers covering 50 square miles. Every traveler who has laid eyes on it has described Rainier as one of the most breathtaking sights in the world. From Port Angeles on the Canadian border, more than 200 miles to the north, its snowy crest dominates the eastern horizon. From Olympia, the state capital, a hundred miles south, it appears like a great white giant crouched against the sky. It has not a single nearby rival—this icy colossus of the vast Pacific Northwest.

Mount Rainier served as a perfect site on which to prepare for a Himalayan attempt. The Americans had spent a week there climbing together, getting to know one another, and testing several tons of new equipment: nylon tents, two-way aluminum pots, oxygen, rope, ice axes, and scores of special foods, including watermelon rind, chutney, smoked oysters, and artichoke hearts. Those morsels might sound like needless luxuries to take to Mount Everest, but there was a reason. The nutritionists theorized that delicacies such as watermelon rind and smoked oysters would spur the climbers to eat adequately when the high altitude depressed their hunger. It was also believed that such rich food would cause the men to crave water, and large amounts of liquid were going to be vitally necessary to stem the weakening effects of high-altitude dehydration.

One thing that Mount Rainier has in common with mighty Mount Everest is snow—more than 83 feet some seasons, piling up drifts deep enough to bury an apartment building, crashing down in avalanches that can wipe out a man in the flick of an eyelash. It also boasts many glaciers—26 of them—more than can be found on any other mountain in the United States. Then, too, Mount Rainier's fickle weather closely resembles that on Mount Everest, the kind that can beset climbers with chilling fog, hot sun, and blinding blizzards, all in the space of only a few hours.

Eighteen of the 20 men Norman Dyhrenfurth signed for the 1963 American Everest Expedition assembled at Mount Rainier's Paradise Inn for the "shakedown" phase of the program. The other two men, Colonel Jimmy Roberts and Dr. Willi Unsoeld, were already in Nepal and would join the expedition when it arrived.

On September 5, the expedition set out under heavy loads for Camp Muir, located at 10,000 feet on Rainier's south slope. Pack horses had already carried up half a ton of food, equipment, and scientific instruments for them the day before.

On the way to Muir the mountaineers all wore a new type of oxygen mask to test it and become accustomed to its use. This vital device was developed by Dr. Tom Hornbein with researchers of the Maytag Company. Vastly superior to masks used on previous missions, it could be de-iced merely by squeezing the flexible exhaust tube, and its simple, one-valve construction made breathing easier and reduced chances of malfunction. "I feel as if I'm wearing Cyrano's nose," grinned Barry Bishop. As they hiked through the fields of flowers near Paradise Inn, the men presented a strange picture to park strollers. "What on earth are you wearing those gas masks for?" they were asked.

Jim Whittaker supervised the testing of clothing, and the little lessons the climbers learned were later to save them all much pain and peril on the slopes of Everest. For instance, they lengthened their down-filled parkas four inches to protect them from cold when they sat in the snow. On Everest they would live constantly in those parkas, even sleeping in them at high altitudes. They changed the pockets to allow easier access to hands in bulky mittens. It was decided to use nylon zippers, lighter than brass and less likely to freeze.

They also discarded a leather climbing boot with opossum-fur insulation because the stitching caused leaks and blisters. They preferred a boot with a removable felt inner sole that was more comfortable and easier to keep dry. This was just one of four types of boots they would need for Everest's varying conditions. Even their tents were modified. One yellow nylon tent material was a delight for photographers, but it transmitted so much light inside the tent that the climbers would have risked snow blindness without dark goggles. The color was changed to deep orange.

To test their ice screws, or "coat hangers," they went up into an area of winding, jumbled crevasses to a high vertical ice face. An ice screw bites into a frozen surface like a corkscrew, and half a dozen of the men attached a climbing rope and tried a tug-of-war against one screw. It wouldn't budge. When the same test was tried with an ordinary piton, or spike, it popped out and sent the climbers sprawling. But the crucial test came when Dick Pownall fastened his climbing rope to three screws at varying heights and jumped off a 40-foot cliff. His trust was not betrayed. The top screw gave way under the force of his fall, but the second one held, stopping him before he hit bottom. Though there was some risk, such tests assured everyone that they had the best mountaineering equipment in the world.

Dick Pownall was also the expedition's food expert, and he had brought to Mount Rainier more than a hundred varieties to test. Most were "freeze-dried," a new process that allows lighter weight and tastier meals. The ten tons of food he selected for Everest included such varied fare as diced chicken, shrimp, beefsteak, and the delicacies mentioned previously. On a high mountain climb every ounce counts, yet the list of paraphernalia the Americans planned for Everest seemed endless. Butane stoves and lanterns, shovels, aluminum ladders, ski poles, insect repellents, signal mirrors, boot wax—these were but a few of the items they would take with them to Everest. Altogether, their equipment and supplies totaled 53,000 pounds.

Stamina and teamwork were going to be extremely important in the high Himalayas, and Mount Rainier gave the men a chance to examine both. They broke up into two- and three-man teams and reviewed ice-climbing techniques.

One of the first considerations in ice climbing is the use of the nylon rope. Supplanting the old-style rope of hemp or Manila—and now used universally—it has proved itself superior in almost every way. It is stronger, more pliable and less subject to kinking and freezing. Its outstanding virtue, however, is its elasticity, which enables it not only to hold a falling man, but to do it with a minimum of damage. The rope commonly used in mountaineering is ⅜ of an inch or 7/16 of an inch in diameter and between 80 and 150 feet long. There are a number of standard knots for tying it around the body—for both end and middle men—and the distance between climbers may vary according to the nature of the ascent. But it is essential that the rope be allowed neither to drag slackly nor to pull jerkily between them. As many as a dozen men have been known to climb on one rope, and as few as two. Modern technique favors smaller groups, with three usually considered the ideal number.

The order of climbing on a rope is of great importance and should be determined carefully according to the dictates of common sense. The man highest on the mountain at any given time is the one who can give the most assistance to his companions. Therefore, on an ascent, the strongest member of a party should always go first; on a descent, last. The weakest member should be last on the ascent, but in the middle on the descent, when it would be inadvisable for him to lead. Too great emphasis cannot be placed on the responsibilities of the top man on a rope. The anchor for all below him, he is himself without anchor (unless pitons are employed), and a slip or misstep on his part can easily result in serious consequences.

When the rope is used simply as a general precaution, all members of a climbing party will usually be in motion at the same time on a routine ascent. On difficult rock, however, the rope becomes an active protective device, and its proper use limits the movements of the group to one man at a time. At such times climbers make use of the protective maneuver known as a belay. The first step in belaying is for the anchor man on a team to take the most secure and protected stance he can find. He then passes the rope around either his own body or a projecting mass of rock, or both, in such a way that a slip or fall by the man actually climbing will put the least possible strain both on the rope and on himself. It is vital that there be no slack between belayer and climber, for this would allow too much momentum to develop before the fall is stopped. The belay should be resilient so that there will be no great jerk, but rather a gradual braking process.

When the climbing grows exceedingly hazardous, it is important for the top man, as well as the others, to have some measure of protection, and here the piton and karabiner (a metal snap ring through which the rope passes for more security) come into play. As he climbs, the leader hammers pitons into cracks in the rock, affixes karabiner and rope, and the rope is then belayed by a fellow climber below.

Another common use of the rope is in the traditional technique of the rappel. It is used only when coming down, allowing a climber to lower himself down cliff faces and overhangs which could not be negotiated by normal methods. For the rappel, or "roping down," a supplementary rope is used, thinner and usually longer than the standard one. This is passed around a rock point or threaded through a firmly fastened rope ring directly above the stretch to be descended, so that two equal lengths hang down the mountain. In the simplest type of rappel in which no extra equipment is required, the climber wraps a fold of the doubled rope around himself, under one thigh, diagonally across the body and over the opposite shoulder, and, facing in toward the mountain, proceeds to lower himself by letting the rope slip through first one hand and then the other. The entire operation is based on the fact that the friction of the rope passing around the body takes almost all strain from the hands and arms. The weight of the rope itself serves as a brake, very powerful at the beginning of a descent when there are still two long strands dangling below the climber, becoming gradually less so as the strands shorten. In the case of steep or even vertical rocks the climber, in effect, walks backward down the mountainside.

Above all, the use of the rope requires close and constant teamwork. Each man must know at all times what the others are doing, for it is the sudden surprise, the unexpected slip, that can carry one man or a whole party to death.

Climbers roped together are often hidden from one another by intervening crags and bulges, and shouting is the only means of communication. For such situations most veteran climbers have developed a sort of shorthand code of speech, so that talk is used only to exchange the necessary instructions and information.

But the success or failure on Mount Everest was going to depend upon much more than going up and down a nylon rope. A true mountaineer must be many things. One moment he is a cragsman, clinging to a dizzy ledge; the next he is a meteorologist studying the barometer; again a homesteader searching for a secure spot to pitch his tent and sleep. The Americans who were preparing to challenge Everest had to be all things: geologist, cartographer, photographer, trail scout, botanist, cook, rope splicer, explorer, guide, follower, philosopher, doctor, friend—and human guinea pig. All would find constant danger and privation, long drudgery and backbreaking work, for Everest was a formidable enemy and its visitors from the West would be given no margin for error. Their fate depended to a great extent upon just how well they had learned their techniques back home.

A series of evening conferences, or skull sessions, were also on the agenda at Rainier, and they involved the numerous scientific experiments planned for Everest. In one discussion, Dr. Will Siri, a biophysicist who was deputy leader of the expedition, warned the men that some of the tests were going to demand great physical and mental stresses on each of them. He told them, "These tests are going to push you to the limits of endurance." He went on to remind them that when men climb to extreme heights, particularly above 22,000 feet, they deteriorate physically and psychologically from the bitter cold, exhaustion, dehydration, and from lack of oxygen. "You will probably lose strength and motivation, become irritable, and will be unable to get to sleep," he cautioned the climbers. "Your appetites will sink, you'll lose weight, and become apprehensive." The effects of these stresses would be studied on Everest.

Dr. Siri's job, along with the three medical doctors, was to conduct physiological tests on the team. With the help of radioactive isotopes he hoped to measure the changes that would take place in their adrenal glands. Dr. Jim Lester would ask them hundreds of questions and probe into their thoughts to

Lute Jerstad in action on Mount Rainier in Washington State. Jerstad has climbed the 14,410-foot peak 41 times; Rainier served as the practice site for the Americans preparatory to going to Everest.

The opening pages of Lute Jerstad's Everest diary.

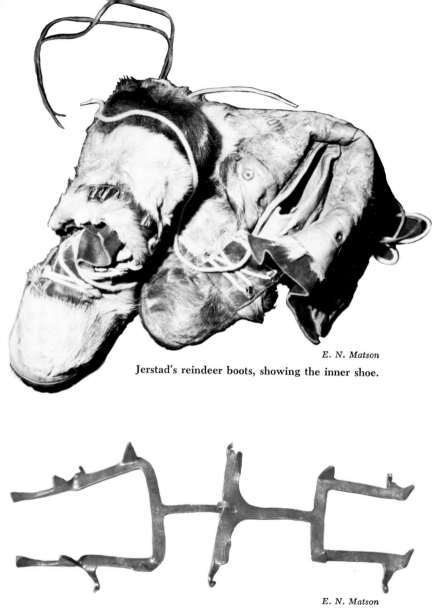

Jerstad's reindeer boots, showing the inner shoe.

Jerstad's crampons.

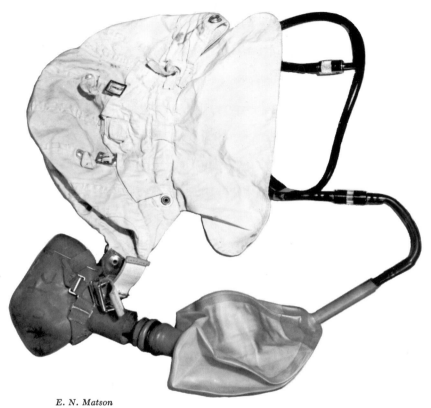

Jerstad's oxygen mask and helmet.

Jerstad's pack, which he was carrying when he stood on the summit of Everest.

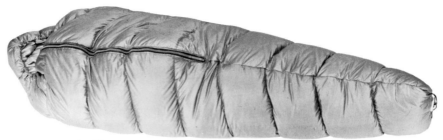

Hodge Photos

Special insulated sleeping bag, designed for sub-zero temperatures, kept the American climbers warm and snug.

Fred Milkie Photographers

Gloves like these kept the climber's hands warm.

Fred Milkie Photographers

One of four kinds of jacket worn by the Everesters.

Windbreakers were worn over quilted trousers like these.

find out what psychological changes took place; and Dr. Dick Emerson, the sociologist, wanted to learn how well they were able to communicate with each other under growing pressure and unrest. He would use lightweight tape recorders so that their conversations and comments could be analyzed after the trip was over.

The weather was warm and sunny during their first four days on Mount Rainier, but then a bitter storm struck the training party's camp with heavy snow and high winds. The future climbers of Everest were pleased, for the blizzard allowed them to conduct additional tests under near-Himalayan conditions. It also reminded the members that the icy wind was going to be their constant foe once the expedition reached the high Himalayas.

But this was a confident party of mountain men, and, barring the supernatural, neither storm nor snow nor subzero temperatures nor the perils of Everest itself was going to keep the Americans from reaching their goals and fulfilling the most ambitious series of objectives in mountaineering history.

3

On to Everest

There were thousands of tasks to be completed, and almost at the same time, before the Americans and 27 tons of cargo could be assembled in Katmandu, the capital of Nepal. That gave them only four months, and there was no Aladdin's lamp at their disposal. The autumn days filed past; then the weeks. And then at last, on January 14, 1963, Barry Bishop, Dan Doody, and Norman Dyhrenfurth boarded a Pan American jet in Los Angeles and flew to Calcutta as the Official Advance Group of the

24

expedition. They left three weeks ahead of the rest of the climbing party to do most of the detail work, such as clearing all red tape through the Foreign Ministry and Central Customs, double-checking their porterage manpower, and inventorying food and equipment.

25

From Calcutta, Norman flew on alone to Katmandu, leaving Barry and Dan behind to travel by road to Patna with the truck convoy carrying the expedition's goods. Norman's plane touched down at Gaucher Airport, a tiny field on the outskirts of Katmandu, where he was met by Colonel Jimmy Roberts, a retired British army officer residing in Nepal. While Jimmy Roberts and Norman spent the next few days with the Foreign Ministry and Customs, Dan and Barry drove with the truck convoy to Patna. From Patna the cargo was airlifted to Katmandu by a DC-3 of Indian Airlines. The first of seven flights was made directly from Calcutta to Katmandu, the others in shorter hops between the capital city and Patna. The entire complicated operation took only three days, with Dan at one end of the line and Norman at the other. Meanwhile, Barry rode the truck carrying all of the oxygen, butane, kerosene and gasoline to Katmandu, since it couldn't be flown in. The journey generally takes about a week, but Barry bulldozed his way through in less than two days, despite the fact that it cost him a day and 850 rupees to clear his cargo through Central Customs. All told, the job was completed on February 12. Truckload after truckload of fuel, oxygen, food and equipment was neatly stacked in high piles in a compound behind Katmandu's Hotel Royal. When the last box had been unloaded, Norman sank into the chair behind his hotel desk, totally exhausted. The first big stage of the advance work was done.

The main body of the American Everest Expedition, 15 strong, had assembled at San Francisco's International Airport on February 2. They had seemed a fairly routine group of travelers, but under the surface they were a concentration of energy, excitement, and anticipation. The roll call included Will Siri, Al Auten, Jake Breitenbach, Barry Corbet, Dave Dingman, Dick Emerson, Tom Hornbein, Lute Jerstad, Jim Lester, Maynard Miller, Dick Pownall, Barry Prather, Gil Roberts, Jim Ullman, and Jim Whittaker.

The next morning they were airborne toward Katmandu. Short stops were made in Hawaii and Wake Island, and then Tokyo, where they met members of the Japanese Alpine Club and saw a special screening of a film made by the 1960 Communist Chinese Everest Expedition. The film was interesting, but it threw no light on the much-doubted Red Chinese claim that they had conquered the summit. From Tokyo, the Americans visited Hong Kong for three days, and Bangkok for two. Another day was spent in Calcutta. Finally, on February 12, a Royal Nepalese Airlines DC-3 took off and bore them northward. Spread beneath them were the brown plains of West Bengal, and presently the wide curving channels of the Ganges. Then, at last, came what they all were waiting for . . .

"There they are!"

Fifteen faces were suddenly pressed against the panes, as the great white wave of the Himalayas rose before them. There they were, all right. Hundreds

27

of them, a horizon filled with them. Some, higher
than others, were easily recognized. Far to the east
there was the sprawling bulk of Kanchenjunga.
Diagonally ahead was Makalu. And beyond Makalu
was IT, their goal: the peak of mighty Mount Everest—rising like a magnificent giant above all the
rest, its snow plume streaming across the cloudless
sky. Some day not too far off, several of them would
have a view of that peak from a very different angle.

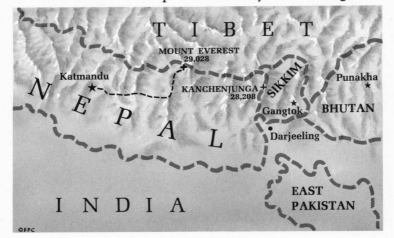

At Katmandu, the whole expedition was united
finally for the first time. Twenty members in all, officially. They included Jimmy Roberts and Willi
Unsoeld. Willi had been in Nepal since the fall of
1962 as an administrative officer with the Peace
Corps, and had been given a leave of absence by
Peace Corps officials in Washington, D.C., to join
the expedition.

28

The expedition established its headquarters at the Hotel Royal, and during the week prior to departure its nerve center was one of the hotel compounds where all the supplies were accumulated in staggering array. Jimmy Roberts, armed with vast expedition experience and a fluent command of the Nepali language, took charge of the cargo, sorting through the mountains of food, clothing, and equipment to see that nothing was missing. Helping him were 37 Sherpas and the Americans themselves.

Everyone worked tirelessly. Norman Dyhrenfurth devoted most of his attention to settling the question of U.S. currency with the Foreign Ministry. The State Department grant provided the expedition with Indian rupees, but the Nepalese government insisted on payment in U.S. dollars for all purchases within Nepal. Heated words were flung back and forth. Prospects of the expedition leaving for Everest on schedule were ticklishly slim, and it appeared very likely that the project would be canceled altogether unless Norman agreed to meet the Nepali demand. The American Ambassador to Nepal stanchly supported Norman and through his unbending efforts the problem was finally solved 24 hours before the scheduled big push. On the eve of departure, Nepal's Chief of Protocol handed Norman the actual written permit to climb Everest. Only then did the Americans breathe a sigh of relief. The second phase of the long-awaited American expedition to Mount Everest was finished.

4

H-Hour

In the parlance of a wartime army, the day a force strikes a new country is called D-day, and the time it hits the beach is H-hour. For the Americans on Everest, D-day was February 20 and H-hour was 11:15 A.M.

The Americans were ready. The Sherpas were ready. The coolie porters were ready. Finally, in single file, the 4-mile-long procession started to move out of a field at Banepa, which marked the end of the road at the eastern end of the Valley of Katmandu.

Men, women, and children porters, bent under their heavy loads, moved up the trail in an unbroken line that took two hours to pass a given point. Each teen-age and adult porter carried a 65-pound pack, to which was added his personal gear: a blanket, a water container, and several days' supply of rice. The children packed loads up to 40 pounds. Some of the women porters carried babies on their packs, and small Lhasa Apso dogs ran up the trail beside their masters. Spaced at wide intervals among the porters marched the Americans, turning, waving, shouting good-by to the hundreds of local citizens from Katmandu who had come to see them off.

The Americans' assault on Everest from the time they left Banepa until they disgorged at Base Camp many days later was largely a matter of logistics. The process of transporting 53,000 pounds of food, oxygen, fuel, and equipment up there was one of the superlative feats of the expedition, for to set out on such a journey, over the highest mountain ranges and into the most remote country in the world, required very careful planning. If they forgot something essential, it was just too bad. There were no hotels or restaurants along the route they were taking. The way was cruel, the weather forbidding, and every pound of those supplies had to be carried up on the backs of people.

On that first day the caravan followed a trail that was never straight. It went up and down, across streams and around hills. But the hikers made surprisingly good time, arriving at Panch-khal, the first overnight stop, at 2:30 P.M. Lute's diary gives us a graphic, on-the-spot account of the scene:

We traveled 5 miles today. It was a fairly easy hike. There is the usual first-day crop of blistered feet. Gombu [head Sherpa] had a particularly hard day of it. He ran a nail into his foot yesterday and it is still very sore. By the time we arrived here this afternoon, the Sherpas already had set up our camp alongside several converging streams, but the pace quickened as soon as Gombu arrived. He's in charge of the Sherpas and acts as an interpreter. He speaks a number of languages. Whole Sherpa families hire out for these expeditions. I saw some 12- and 13-year-old kids carrying 65-pound loads today, plus about 10 pounds of their own gear. They are fantastic. . . . This is big country; country so big that, in the clear air of early dawn or late evening, one can see farther in one glance than he could hope to travel in a whole day; and in all the miles between here and Base Camp, except for the Sherpa villages up ahead, we will see little evidence that we are still part of an inhabited world.

The Americans knew that Everest was plagued with avalanches and precipices and great walls of rock and ice. Nor were they ignorant of the fact that Everest rose from the heart of a remote and almost inaccessible wilderness, necessitating not only great physical endurance in those who challenged the pinnacle, but elaborate arrangements for supply, transport, and communication. They also knew that, once the mountain was reached, there would be the constant question of weather. The climates of India and Tibet are almost as unlike as those of the Equator and the Poles, the result being that Everest is a battleground of conflicting winds. Central Asia pours gale winds down from the west and north, while from India and the tropical seas beyond flow the warm, damp air currents that culminate each summer in the feared monsoon. The Americans recognized the monsoon as their most treacherous and relentless enemy. The difference between triumph and disaster was going to be a matter of beating those drenching rainstorms that annually turned the heights of Everest into vast death traps of melting, crumbling snow. They had only about three and a half months to get the job done.

There was also the problem of living and functioning properly at altitudes where the air contained only a fraction of the oxygen required by climbers. Among the resultant hazards for them would be the high-altitude sickness known as pulmonary edema. Consequently, they would be expected to undergo a period of gradual acclimatizing before their bodies adjusted to the change. Serious bodily deterioration would set in if too much time was spent at heights where the air was extremely thin. Neither age, strength, nor physical condition was going to prove to be a particularly reliable criterion of individual performance, because men vary greatly in their speed and degree of acclimatization. So there was no way to safely estimate which Americans would stand up and which ones would crack once the expedition reached the high country.

In his diary, Lute pondered the problem of mountain sickness and how the climbers would react individually to the substratosphere:

From experience and all we have read and been told, the critical altitude for high-altitude sickness is usually about 14,000 feet. If one isn't sick at that height, he probably will not be sick, except in the event of great exertion, until he passes his own effective altitude. The key to avoiding sickness, of course, is to move up slowly, acclimatizing ourselves gradually. If, for example, we were suddenly dropped from an airplane on top of Everest without oxygen masks on, we would be dead in about ten minutes—that's how serious it can be. Mountain sickness does not always come over a climber suddenly. Nor does it always start with nausea or headaches or dizziness. It may start with a feeling of great exhilaration, as if intoxicated. But altitude, like alcohol, sometimes gives a false sense of strength, power, and poise.

The expedition's initial goal—acclimatization camp, a few miles southwest of Everest—had an altitude of 14,000 feet. At such heights the air contains only about half as much oxygen per breath as at sea level. A man breathes faster and deeper, the chest enlarges, the heart pumps more blood, the blood carries more oxygen. Much carbon dioxide is exhaled. Errors in calculation that seem ridiculous at sea level are common. Memory fails and there is a tendency to argue. It was not a pretty prospect.

Acclimatization camp lay 160 miles up the trail. But the terrain in between by no means was going to be a straight 10,000-foot shot uphill. The caravan's progress for the next 10 days was going to be up and down, down and up, from valley to ridge, ridge to valley through the Himalayan foothills.

On the debit side of the first day's march was the loss of Jim Ullman, who, at 55, was the oldest member of the American team. His recuperation from two operations for circulatory trouble had been disappointingly slow, and after examining him at Panch-khal the expedition doctors refused to give him permission to travel farther.

At 4 o'clock the next morning the porters were stirring. By 6 o'clock they were on their way. By 8 o'clock the whole of the expedition was gone. Jim Ullman had watched them go with emotions impossible to describe. He would go back to Katmandu and do his best to carry out his duties as historian of the expedition, nursing the fond hope that he would eventually feel up to rejoining his teammates. In the meantime, it was going to be a long, long wait before runners brought back news from the advancing climbers.

Tashi delai! Jim Ullman thought to himself in Sherpa as he watched the last of the caravan drift out of sight up the twisting trail. "Here's how! And may you all have good fortune."

5

The Sherpas

The Americans could not have tolerated Everest's many changing moods without the help of those semi-nomadic hillmen—the Sherpas. Their peculiar physiology is made to order for the Himalayas. They first made their appearance in Everest activities in the 1920s, and since that date scarcely a major Himalayan expedition has dared start without them. To call them "guides" would be incorrect in the special Alpine sense of the word, nor would it be proper to call them porters or coolies. Their rightful designation falls somewhere in between, because in recent years they have been regarded as genuine mountaineers who have gone with their heavy loads as far up the great peaks as the professional climbers themselves. The Americans recognized them as an indomitable breed, able to throw off disappointment and discouragement. They seldom complained. They recognized the presence of danger but were not deterred by it.

On the approach march the Americans paired off, and a Sherpa was assigned to each two-man tent. Teaming up with Lute was Jake Breitenbach. Their personal Sherpa was named Nima Tensing. Lute's impressions of the Sherpas are contained in his diary:

February 21: This is our second day on the trail. The Sherpas are serving us well. They help us carry our loads, pitch our tents, prepare our food, build campfires, blow up our air mattresses, and spread out our sleeping bags. We have 16 aluminum camp chairs with us and look like "Ugly Americans." Sherpas bring our food to a table we've brought with us and we sit there eating like kings; this temporary luxury will disappear shortly, however, when we reach the mountain. Today I hiked part of the way with our head Sherpa, Nawang Gombu. He's the nephew of Tenzing [who scaled Everest with Sir Edmund Hillary in 1953]. What is known of Sherpa history is extremely interesting. They came originally from southern Tibet and migrated to Nepal and the vicinity of Darjeeling. Born and bred in mountain villages of from 10,000 to 13,000 feet, they adjust to high altitudes easily. They are very religious and pray a great deal; on the trail the predawn calm is often stirred by the chanting from Sherpa tents. They used to be a superstitious race, believing in Bön Shamanism, but with the arrival of Buddhism they have grown more sophisticated in their thinking. They are not intellectual giants by any stretch of the imagination—in fact, few of them can read or write—but they are intelligent men. Physically, they stand on the average between 5 feet 4 and 5 feet 6 inches and weigh about 125 pounds; they are deep- but not broad-chested, with well-muscled necks and shoulders but thin arms. They have pale brown skin, not dark, and their hair is coal black. It is very amusing to hike alongside Jim Whittaker, for all the villagers point and giggle at his 6-foot-5-inch frame. He is a giant for this part of the world. Gombu told me that some villagers had remarked to him about how much meat they could get out of our well-fed legs!

The expedition clicked off 35 miles in the first three days. Conditions for hiking were ideal, dry and fairly cool. On the night of February 22, they camped at Risingo, and Lute, footsore and weary, recorded his impressions in his diary:

Starting at 6:30 A.M., we really burned up the trail today. I traveled with Gombu and Nima Tensing; no grass grows under their feet. They really hustle. I am not in shape yet and like a fool I tried to keep up with them. I did it but almost ran myself into the ground. It is too early in the game for that fast a pace. At noon we stopped long enough for a refreshing dip in a nearby stream, and the native porters, curious, crowded offshore to gawk. They can't figure out the strange Americans. Whenever we sit down to eat or to relax in our lawn chairs, the coolies come up and stand in front of us and stare. They show no emotion whatsoever. They don't seem to resent us, it's just that we are *different*. Jimmy Roberts has charge of the Sherpas and manages them beautifully. He speaks Nepali fluently but not Sherpa, while the most prominent languages among the natives are Sherpa, Newari, Nepali, and English. I believe that if put to the test some of the I.Q. numbers of the Sherpas would be quite high. They possess keen memories and can remember such minute details as where something is packed in the more than 900 boxes we have brought with us. Risingo is a lamasery village and we are camped right in the front yard. We will probably have the dubious pleasure of listening to weird Lama music tonight. Dr. Jim Lester [psychologist of the expedition] has started keeping track of our dreams. He wants a full detailed report of all we dream about. I stay awake half the night now worrying that I'll forget the dream I just had! Dick Emerson has us all keeping little diaries. . . . The group still gets along quite well together; no blowups yet.

The weather remained wonderfully cool the next day, and, crossing the tops of the low ridges, one could look to the north and see the white peaks of the Himalayas. But not Everest. It would remain hidden to the east, behind lesser peaks, until the expedition was almost there. Yet what they did see was more than enough for the time being. Like the

Hindu and Buddhist generations before them who had traveled the same trail, they were pilgrims raising their eyes to the distant snows. At this point, Lute's diary, on a more mundane level, reveals some of the physical difficulties they encountered en route to Base Camp:

Drinking water is becoming a problem. A few of us are suffering from severe dysentery. It hits and runs; strikes you for half a day and then disappears. Right now I feel like rolling over in a grave. We have passed some nice clear streams along the trail but dare not drink out of them because of the villages higher up. The natives use them for sewage disposal! Both Jim Lester and Al Auten are hurting from terrible blisters on their feet. Tonight we are camped at Chitare, on a ridge 7,500 feet high. The sun has gone behind the clouds and we are wearing our down-underwear tops. This afternoon, however, it was very warm, causing the porters to whistle like a teapot on a stove, something they do when they are tired. Music bolsters their spirits, so we sing and whistle, too; at one rest stop I took out my ukulele and played for them. At Risingo, the Sherpas put on some of their native dances. It was quite interesting. Nima Tensing did a dance with grimaces and facial twitches—I don't know what it was supposed to represent. Another dance depicted a boy and girl looking at themselves in a mirror. These breaks help to ease tensions. The porters have been working hard and a couple of them got into a fist-fight this afternoon. Al Auten and Dan Doody came up the trail just as four or five porters were beating one guy with their sticks. Al and his

Sherpas jumped in and broke it up. The beaten porter had large welts on his back and his wind had been knocked out. Al got one accidental rap on the knee for his trouble. We are camped at about 7,500 feet tonight, the highest we've been yet. My air mattress went flat twice last night and I spent a rather uncomfortable night. We came across a cremation today at the spot where we ate lunch. They burned the body right on the river bank.

Despite the usual early crop of sore feet, blisters, and touches of dysentery, the Americans continued to make good progress. Every day of that first week found them reaching higher ground, where they reveled in cooler weather and in the constantly changing countryside. Terraced hillsides gave way to more sinister slopes and to rickety swinging foot bridges extending across wild streams. The following excerpt from Lute's diary was written at a tiny village called Kirantichhap:

We had to cross a chain-link bridge over a small gorge today, and it swayed and rattled under the weight. Many of our porters refused to cross it and waded the stream instead. We parked along the stream for breakfast and Whittaker and I went swimming and washed clothes. We were still in the water when a porter lost his yak-skin boot, and Jim and I tried to get it for him. Jim got to it first, but went under just as I stumbled over some rocks. Without exaggeration, it was touch and go there for a few minutes and provoked much excitement. Will

Siri came down with a recurrence of bursitis in his left shoulder and is in quite a bit of pain. I seem to be getting over my dysentery but have a bad cold yet. I am still somewhat weak. Dr. Schnitzler, a Ph.D. in political science from U.C.L.A., is hiking with us. Whittaker and I had a long talk with him about the political future of Nepal. If China decides to move again, the Nepalese situation won't be too bright. A few days ago we stopped to eat at a place located just across the river from where a Chinese Communist work crew was building a new road and bridge to be "donated" to Nepal. A uniformed policeman walked guard, and he sent over to us an English-written message demanding we take no pictures. With the completion of this new road the Communists will be in a position to launch a three-pronged attack against India. We could very well be the last Western expedition allowed to come in here.

Yersa, which sits on a concave hillside overlooking a barren, terraced rice paddy, was the next stop, on February 26:

This has been a tough day for the porters. Up, down —up, down. We dropped from 4,500 feet to 2,900 feet on the Bhota Kosi, crossed another narrow footbridge, then climbed clear to 6,200 feet. We began marching at 6 A.M. (we're starting out earlier every morning now—Corbet figures we'll be arising at 2 A.M. by the time we reach Thyangboche) and the sun hid behind clouds most of the way here, so it was quite cool. We crossed the Bhota Kosi this morning on a very fine bridge for this part of the world. The Bhota Kosi originates in Tibet and is quite a large river. Anullu [a Sherpa] arrived tonight with six porters carrying the late shipment from Calcutta and some mail. A Yersa woman who apparently feels she owns the ground we are camping on tonight was screaming a while ago about our porters stealing her wood. She was furious. She beat on a couple of them and then called down the wrath of the gods upon the rest of us. Everybody just ignored her. I can sympathize with her though, living way out here, when suddenly some 900 people show up out of nowhere and begin crawling all over the area like ants.

From Yersa on, Everest's resistance to the Americans increased; and all along the trail personalities emerged from the fabric of the Sherpa corps. These gallant men knew little about the New World, but they were vital cogs in the daily life of the expedition. If the Americans had any complaints, it was that their adopted brothers were too proficient. The extent of their competence can be gauged by this passage from Lute's diary:

We kid about how efficient our Sherpas are. They are so blamed efficient, as a matter of fact, that they cause minor problems. Yesterday, for example, Dan Doody threw away a letter he'd been carrying—and today Passang Temba, his personal Sherpa, handed it back to him. Then Will Siri tore out the hot lining of his *terai* hat and threw it away. When he opened his pack the next morning—there was his hat lining, neatly tucked back in his hat. If we throw anything away we have to bury it. This afternoon Barry Cor-

THE ROUTE FROM
KATMANDU TO EVEREST

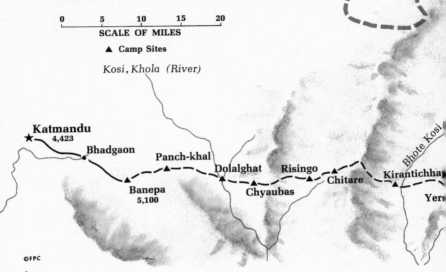

```
0      5     10     15     20
SCALE OF MILES
▲ Camp Sites
```

Kosi, Khola (River)

Katmandu
★ 4,423
    Bhadgaon
              Panch-khal
                    Dolalghat   **Risingo**
Banepa   **Chyaubas**   **Chitare**   **Kirantichha**
5,100   **Yers**

Bhote Kosi

©FPC

bet had clothes washed by his Sherpa—and he hadn't even worn them yet!

On February 27 the expedition spent the night at Those, population 500, where Lute recorded:

This is a rather large village for this far back in the country. It has a food store, a clothes shop, and a school. A young teacher from the Katmandu Valley met us at the village and showed us his outdoor school. The town is building a new school house. The Sherpas continue to amaze us. I lost a rubber

bag with a letter to my folks in it. I told Nima Tensing about losing it and a half hour later he found it
300 yards away! A funeral procession passed by camp
and blew some very long, loud horns in our direction.
I mistakenly thought we were being serenaded by
townspeople. I hunted half the night for my head-
lamp and discovered in the morning that Nima had
attached it to my pack for easy access. The foliage
around here is somewhat like eastern Washington,
with pine trees and open countryside. Spending the
night here at Those is like a fancy night in the "big
city" for our porters. Many of them have been dip-

45

ping into the chang, a native beer of reputed strength. There are going to be some unsteady legs and splitting heads when we hit the trail in the morning.

The route to Chyangma, their next stop, led them deeper into wilderness. It was an eroded trail in places, fringed with trees and rockbound cliffs. Lute wrote in his diary:

This is our ninth day out and we are really getting into the higher mountains now. We can *feel* them the more we advance. The nights are growing colder. We crossed a 9,000-foot pass this afternoon, and from this point we'll not drop below 6,000 feet for three months. The day after tomorrow we cross a 12,000-foot pass, which is visible from here with snow on it. Unsoeld, Emerson, and Hornbein have been working daily on the horrendous task of figuring logistics for the mountain via both the West Ridge and the South Col routes. What a job! The Sherpas brought some chang for us, but I'm afraid we must acquire a taste for it. It is lumpy and muddy-looking. We didn't drink much of it.

On the morning of March 1, a series of mishaps, any one of which might have been fatal, began rasping nerves already drawn taut by the growing demands of rougher terrain:

At 9:15 A.M. we were at our breakfast site when Nima Tensing came running into camp with the information that the chain bridge, about one and a half miles back, had collapsed and 11 porters were hurt. We all took off immediately for the bridge. Norman and Dan Doody had been shooting movies, and Norman had just moved from under the bridge when it caved in with the porters on it. Norman missed severe injury by the narrowest of margins. The porters fell about 20 feet onto rocks and into the stream. Several were carried downriver with their loads and were fished out by Norman and some Sherpas. Eight of them were really hurt, suffering bad bruises, lacerations, and shock. One was a possible thigh-fracture case, but all walked later. Our doctors took over and patched them up. The injured porters were really tough and walked uphill for three hours after the spill—an amazing feat. Their pride is something to be desired and envied. Tomorrow is going to be a hard day for them as we must climb to a height of 12,000 feet (4,500 feet from here) and then drop down again to 10,000 feet to Junbesi.

At Junbesi, on March 2, the diary continues:

We hit snow today. Our Tamang porters from the Katmandu Valley are mostly barefoot and they went right through the 12,000-foot pass, snow and all. We dropped about 2,000 feet and are at a lamasery village called Junbesi, a beautiful place nestled in a valley with hills all around. Barry Corbet got ill during the night and spent a rough day having to climb and descend. There are other problems, too. Sick people all along the trail keep seeking help from our doctors, who never turn them down. The most pathetic case was encountered here today involving a badly burned woman. She had tried to rescue a yak from

47

a flaming shed and suffered 20 percent burns on her face and arms. Gil [Dr. Roberts] said she would die if we didn't get her to the hospital at Katmandu. That meant digging into our already slim budget for $2,000 or so to hire a helicopter to come and get her. We are hoping the chopper gets up here tomorrow so we can get her out.

The expedition left Junbesi bright and early the following morning, and the Nepalese-Hindu world of the valley gradually sank below; in its place appeared the Sherpa-Buddhist world of the mountains. The climbers stopped to rest at a clearing in the trail below Taksindhu, and Lute took advantage of the break to write:

We had a rather trying night. Porters were camped right beside us, praying, coughing, and talking. At about 10:30, Whittaker suddenly got sick and vomited all over the tent, bags—and us! He was in a bad way all night, but felt better today. The helicopter came and picked up the burned woman this morning. Gil and Dave Dingman said they were helpless in such a severe case. She is salvageable, but her relatives wouldn't even begin carrying her out, so the expedition has to pay for the helicopter. A human life means very little in this part of the world. We crossed Taksindhu Col at 9,600 feet today, where on a clear day we could have seen Everest, but it was cloudy. We were able to see the tops of some 22,000-foot mountains. From the col we dropped through a kind of magnolia-tree jungle with a lot of moss on the trees. A fight broke out as a Sherpa from Solu got drunk on chang, and our Sherpas beat him up slightly and tied him up during the night. They had a "holier-than-thou" look this morning and would admit nothing.

The 37 special Sherpas assumed command of the coolie porters and solved such problems as how to control 908 non-English-speaking porters. Their methods often seemed brutal and unorthodox, but the Americans learned to keep their noses out of porterage affairs. Loads always arrived on schedule, and if there were any serious rank-and-file complaints, the Americans seldom heard of them.

At Kharikhola, Lute wrote:

Jake, Whittaker, Corbet, Bishop, and I are sharing a big five-man tent, and today we finally found out why it's always the first one up. Nima Tensing has been slipping a cigarette to the porter who carries our tent. The porters are allotted only four cigarettes a day, so for one lousy extra smoke a day the coolie breaks his back. Our Sherpas really look out for us. If we try to carry too much, our Sherpa will come along and lighten the pack. They want us to have something left for the mountain. We have earned the Sherpas' respect by doing our share of the work, however. The Sherpas tell us: "Americans good sahibs—strong sahibs—make summit."

There were runny noses, sore throats, and aching bowels, but morale remained high and the complicated machinery of the tedious approach march— hiking and camping, hiking and camping—fell into routine activity. Life's major components of food,

49

shelter, and transport continued under control. On March 5, two days from Namche Bazar, Lute inscribed:

Pownall has the mysterious "bug" tonight just as Whittaker had it. It is like a ghost story with a phantom illness and creates many opportunities for jokes. Snow was quite low on the hills around us this morning, in some places as much as two feet. We have now turned northward after twelve and a half days of eastern travel and are heading up the Dudh Kosi to Namche Bazar. This river drains the Everest group of mountains. It rained heavily during the afternoon and lightning filled the sky. The rain poured buckets for three or four hours but our tents held up well, though there was some leakage.

Namche Bazar, a key Sherpa village, was close at hand now. There some 300 of the low-level porters would be paid off and released and more high-altitude porters hired to help the expedition carry loads as far as Base Camp at 17,800 feet.

The Americans, by early March, had successfully coped with pneumonia and other diseases, but almost all of them were half sick with what Dr. Siri described as "an array of joint disorders, gastrointestinal disturbances, and respiratory infections unknown to medical science and hence untreatable."

Now as they moved higher and higher into the freezing world of ice and snow, beyond modern conveniences and comforts, the invaders from America began to suffer headaches and nausea from the altitude and increasing cold, and at night they would hunch in their sleeping bags with coughing fits. They slept with the aid of pills, even then waking up at intervals gasping for breath.

It was on the afternoon of March 7, several hours down the trail from Namche Bazar, when Jerstad and his companions first got a brief glimpse of Everest's final pyramid from the ground up. And it was then, with the shocked realization that his confidence was slipping away, that Lute started asking himself if he had stamina and courage enough to try for the summit. Suddenly he felt very humble and insignificant. Suddenly he wondered if they should even be there at all.

6

Base Camp: The Nerve Center

The expedition stopped over at Namche Bazar for only two days, March 7–8, the time required to hire a few hundred fresh porters to help the party get its heavy loads up to the Base Camp site. Some of the Americans took advantage of the pause to relax and get acquainted with the villagers. On the second night, Lute wrote:

We climbed up a little hill behind the village here to take pictures of Everest today. A huge plume of snow was blowing off the summit. An incredible sight. Afterward, Siri, Bishop, Whittaker, and I went with Gombu to Sherpa homes to buy rugs. I bought three for 150 rupees each; the same patterns cost 500 to 600 rupees at Katmandu. I also purchased some very nice Tibetan boots. Spent a total of 530 rupees. At each house we had to drink three cups of chang, or at least accept three fillings. By the time we had visited six or seven homes our vision was getting pretty blurry. We move up to Thyangboche tomorrow.

From Namche Bazar to the Base Camp site was a hike of some 23 miles. The elevation rose sharply 5,100 feet over the route they were going and most of the travel resolved itself into one long despairing struggle up terrain as difficult as any in the world. Beyond Namche Bazar were several tiny mountain villages hidden among the hills, appearing no bigger than the dots on a map in a geography book. They would serve as overnight stops for the human baggage train as it slowly wound its way up the mountain en route to the 17,800-foot site where Base Camp would be established, about 2,000 feet below the nightmarish jumble of ice known as the Khumbu Icefall. The icefall represented the "doorway" to the Main Summit of Everest.

Thyangboche was the next stop, March 9. There Jerstad wrote in his diary:

It snowed all last night at Namche Bazar and we had about four inches to slog through this morning to get here. As a result it slowed us down considerably. Bishop, Corbet, Emerson, Hornbein, and I came by way of Khumjung. That's where Sir Edmund Hillary built his school for Sherpas. It was closed today because most of Khumjung was at Namche Bazar either carrying loads or just watching us. It began to snow as we started up here and has kept it up. It could be tough on our porters tomorrow. We had an audience with the High Lama at the lamasery here and were given a tour of the place. We are sleeping in a hut tonight, built by the lamas, and it sure beats tents in this weather.

Lute spent a restless night. Snow blew through the cracks of the hut and the howling of the wind kept him awake. His stomach was upset the next morning, but, fortunately for him, the heavy snow prevented the expedition from advancing, and he took advantage of the indefinite delay to stay inside the hut and try to catch some sleep. He felt much better when he woke up later in the afternoon. The snow continued all day and piled up in drifts two-feet high. Lute described the details in his diary:

We got our first weather report from the Indian weather bureau in Delhi right on schedule today. I spent much of the day sleeping and the rest of the fellows sat around playing cards or reading and hoping for the weather to clear. It began to clear up at 7:30 tonight; the moon came up, and it was one of the most beautiful sights I have ever seen. We held a meeting tonight and tentatively selected our forthcoming climbers for the various routes. I am on the South Col team. Most of the experienced Himalayan

Luther G. Jerstad, AMEE

Chain bridges crossed the rivers and streams in the lower regions on the route to Everest. The Americans and Sherpas often stopped to bathe and do their laundry.

Luther G. Jerstad, AMEE

Human baggage train of low level porters, Sherpas and Americans extended up the trail single-file for 4 miles going from Banepa to Risingo.

Norman G. Dyhrenfurth, AMEE

This magnificent view of Everest, taken at 20,000 feet on Pumori by expedition leader Norman G. Dyhrenfurth, reveals the challenge to the climbers. At top right is the peak of Laotse. In the foreground, flanking the Khumbu Icefall, are the bases of Pumori (left) and Nuptse (right). The location of Base Camp is indicated in the white circle.

Luther G. Jerstad, AMEE

At Lobujya the Expedition halted for acclimatization before going on to Base Camp.

Barry C. Bishop, © National Geographic Society

Dr. Tom Horbein demonstrates the oxygen mask he devised with researchers of the Maytag Company. Worn here by the Sherpas, it proved vastly superior to masks used on previous missions.

In single file, the Americans and Sherpas look like ants as they work their way through the Khumbu Icefall, a chaos of grinding ice and falling snow where Jake Breitenbach lost his life.

The route through the icefall was slow and dangerous.

Scaling Mount Everest is not for the faint-hearted. Here Jerstad inches his way across a narrow bridge of poles. There was no margin for error under such conditions.

Hot meals and hot liquids kept the climbers going. Here Jerstad, right, prepares lunch over a butane stove. The climbers took turns cooking once they left Base Camp, where Sherpa cooks took care of meals.

Jerstad, sitting in the middle, and fellow Everesters relax in a huge recreation tent and catch up on their diaries and letter-writing and reading. Storms often kept the climbers inside for days at a time.

James W. Whittaker, AMEE

The Sherpas, specialists at high climbing, take a break after reaching Camp 4 on the first assault on the summit.

climbers are on the West Ridge team. Some of our loads are still at Namche Bazar and will be brought up by yak tomorrow. Half of the new porters we hired at Namche Bazar will make two relays to Pheriche for us. We will move up there tomorrow if the clear weather holds.

The weather remained unpredictable, however, and by morning it seemed to be deteriorating. There was no choice but to stay on at Thyangboche until there was a change in the outlook. From Jerstad's diary:

We expect to spend the first four days of acclimatization here now and then move on up to Lobujya for another week of acclimatizing. Lobujya is located at about 16,000 feet. We issued equipment today and will spend tomorrow issuing other gear and fitting crampons. The next day we hope to do some climbing. The mail runner came today, a nice surprise. He hooked a ride from Katmandu to Junbesi in the helicopter that flew out the burned Nepalese woman. It was good hearing from home after a delay of two weeks.

The next morning the Americans were awakened by weird sounds of loud horns and clanging gongs coming from the monastery, and Lute supposed the lamas were scaring off the gods or some such. It seemed a strange way to meet the day.

Dave Dingman and Lute set out after breakfast on what is described in the diary as "a nice refreshing walk":

We scrambled a little way up a peak beside camp to almost 14,000 feet. We plan to climb the rest of it tomorrow. It is about 16,000 feet and very easy. We issued crampons today to the sahibs and Sherpas. . . . The yaks came up from Namche Bazar today and still have six more loads to bring. The snow was so heavy at Namche Bazar they had to go through Khumjung. We opened a case of Scotch tonight and will celebrate a little with two bottles—medication, you know!

On March 13, the expedition was still at Thyangboche, and Jerstad wrote:

Today Dingman and I tried to climb the mountain behind camp. Jake [Breitenbach], Dick [Emerson], and Al [Auten] went up another ridge on the 16,000-foot-high peak. We ran into very deep snow—up to our waists for about five hours. Dave and I both felt great and would have continued, except the weather closed in. We had a wonderful time. We had dinner tonight at the High Lama's home. We were very crowded in his little dining room. Our cook handled the meal and lamas served it. We signed his register book.

For Lute this was a strange world. The hand of modern civilization had seldom touched Thyangboche and, as was the tradition of the Sherpa-Buddhist world, sacred religious symbols lined the trails and prayer flags fluttered from the ridges. But the villagers made the Americans feel welcome, and their primitive hospitality was a refreshing change of tempo after more than three weeks on the trail. The diary continues:

I spent a poor night last night. Jake [Breitenbach] had a real coughing spell for hours. He coughed until about 1 A.M. and I didn't get to sleep until about 2 A.M. He feels better today. We issued five extra gear allotments to five new Sherpas today and got most of the gear repacked for transport tomorrow. The new Sherpas are very young, 16 to 19, and have never been on an expedition. It gives them a chance to break into the ranks. They are a pretty select group of men around here and for a boy to start is a real honor. We culled out clothing to be left here for the return march and packed our mountain gear. We still haven't gotten through to Katmandu by radio. They should be listening down there, but no response. We spent about two hours filling out psychology forms and went through a blood-pressure test from Will [Dr. Siri]. My pressure and pulse are higher, of course, than at lower elevation, but not bad—about 125 over 78-85.

After sitting at Thyangboche for six days, the expedition finally moved to Pheriche on March 15:

The weather was good, clear and cold. Ice on the trail made it a little touchy early this morning, however. We climbed through the tiny village of Pangboche and above the timber line. Pheriche is located 14,000 feet high in the Sola Khola Valley. We saw the moraine of the Khumbu Glacier for the first time today. Tomorrow we move on to Lobujya at 16,000 feet and will spend five days or so there. I would like to climb Lobujya peak from there, which is 20,000 feet high and a beautiful mountain. Still have my sore throat. I coughed and sputtered all the way up here. Dave Dingman gave me some penicillin pills to try. I feel good except for the cough.

On the morning of March 16, the marchers hiked from Pheriche to Lobujya in six hours. Lute's cold grew steadily worse and he had a splitting headache. His throat was so sore he could barely swallow. The congestion in his chest slowed him down considerably. Lobujya is 2,000 feet higher than Pheriche, and in some places the way is steep. Lute felt at times as if he would drop in his tracks. Exhaustion sent him stumbling into his tent that evening; his eyes were red with fatigue and coughing, and he gave a silent prayer that he would feel better after a good night's sleep.

Evidence of his lingering cold is revealed in his entry of March 17:

I awoke this morning feeling bad again. My throat was raw and I had a terrible headache. The cooks served us tea in our sleeping bags this morning, which was most welcome. My air mattress went flat during the night, the temperature dropped to 2 degrees, and I spent a miserable time. Despite my condition, I took a hike up the moraine with some of the fellows this morning and saw the Khumbu Icefall, Lho La Pass, Pumori, Changtse, and several other peaks. Some exploratory work will be tried tomorrow. We plan to occupy Base Camp around the 21st of March.

The following morning, March 18, 25 Sherpas and a group of Americans headed for Base Camp with preliminary loads of supplies and equipment. But Jerstad was not with them. He stayed behind to nurse his sore throat. He wrote in his diary, "It hurts to stay behind." The Base Camp advance party got only as far as the old Swiss Lake Camp of 1952, listed on the map as Gorak Shep. There they dropped their loads and returned to Lobujya. The diary explains the shuttle plan:

Loads will first be carried to Gorak Shep by porters and then we will establish regular Base Camp at about 17,800 feet. The porters will relay loads from Gorak Shep to Base Camp. All the guys and Sherpas returned to Lobujya tonight very tired. The snow is soft and thus is tough going for anyone. Some Sherpa porters carried up wood for the cook kitchen. They get twelve rupees a day for a load of wood carried up here.

March 19 was a day of rest for most of the climbers and they sat around camp at Lobujya fussing over their personal gear, checking out radio equipment, drilling extra holes in goggles for ventilation, and in general preparing for the hour when they would move on up to Base Camp. Jerstad writes:

We are all sitting around taking it relatively easy today. I feel better than yesterday but still have a sore throat. Some mail came through today with some vaccine for smallpox. Gil vaccinated the

59

Sherpas and will work on the porters when they arrive. The boy porter who had smallpox back at Ghat died before reaching Katmandu. Two other porters died of it also, so it was a real scare. The burned woman we had flown back to the hospital at Katmandu is doing okay, but I guess we were rather scorned by the Nepalese for being very silly spending all that money for only one life. A life means very little here. The temperature was down to 20 below zero last night. Today the sun is out warmly—about 45 degrees in the sun; air temperature is only 26, however.

March 20 was another day of arduous travel, and this time Lute was with the climbers when they arrived at Gorak Shep, the last stop before Base Camp. The shuttle system was in full swing now as 160 porters carried loads to the old Swiss Camp and returned to Lobujya for more. At least two more round trips per porter were required before all the equipment and supplies were brought up from Lobujya. The same number of trips would then be needed to get all those tons from Gorak Shep to Base Camp—a distance of 800 steep feet. Jerstad tells in his diary of the mounting pressures:

Tomorrow Unsoeld, Whittaker, Dyhrenfurth, Siri, and I are to occupy Base Camp, and the day after that do a reconnaissance of the Khumbu Icefall. It will be tough moving up to two new heights two days in a row. I am quite tired now and am not acclimatized too well and have a sore throat yet and laryngitis. I do want to go up but don't want to jeopardize the reconnaissance. Meanwhile, Corbet and Hornbein are going to try a two-day climb of a rock pinnacle tomorrow across the Khumbu from here. This is a very nice campsite. As spring wears on it will turn green and the lake will have flowers around it.

Aside from logistics and the occasional accidents and minor sicknesses that plague mountaineering operations, the outstanding problem in any campaign is the terrible weariness that builds up inside the men. They soon become exhausted, in mind as well as in body. They acquire a weariness that is mixed with boredom, impatience, fatigue, and loneliness. To sum it all up: a man simply gets sick of it all. After weeks of preliminary activity, he passes the point of known human weariness. He keeps going largely because the other fellow does and because he knows that each man represents an important link in the overall plan of attack. Therefore, despite his nagging cold, Lute was with Norman Dyhrenfurth, Will Siri, Willi Unsoeld, and Jim Whittaker when they shoved off to establish Base Camp on the morning of March 21.

That night Jerstad wrote:

Well, we are finally here. Fifteen Sherpas carried with us but only four stayed. The others have gone back down for more loads. Weather was nice all day. The Sherpas broke trail and we all carried loads. We are established in Base Camp at 17,800 feet, which is way past the old Swiss and British camp and above the Indian camp, which had been the highest until now. We look directly into the icefall and can see

61

the summit of Lhotse. From here the icefall looks quite friendly, but it remains to be seen what happens tomorrow when we go up there and begin putting a route through. We feel good about our chances and hope to make considerable headway the first day. Norman and Will are going up on a slope of Lho La to help direct us up through the maze of ice blocks.

Lute, Jim Whittaker, and Willi Unsoeld shared a four-man tent that night. Lute's eyes remained open in the darkness long after the others had fallen asleep as he thought about the dangers immediately ahead. He knew that risks, psychological as well as physical, were going to be involved from this point on. A person inhabiting the fierce world they were entering had to be prepared to endure the bitter temperatures, killing winds, and isolation which could cause weaker men to crack. Against cold the climber has simple but ample defenses; against the accidents which are inevitable he must trust his luck and inbred ingenuity; but against loneliness and impatience he has nothing much but his own dignity.

Lute made a silent vow to himself that, above all else, he would not lose his dignity when the chips were down.

7

Tragedy at the Icefall

When you look at the Himalayas in color pictures, they seem to roll away before the eye, hazy purple and misty. They seem to be gentle, rolling hills. But the rocks and the cliffs and the snow-choked slopes are there, with outlines blurred by distance. It is no place for a tourist out on a Sunday stroll.

On the morning of March 22, at 9:15, a small procession of five men—three Americans and two Sherpas—left Base Camp and began threading their way among the growing peaks and deepening gorges to pioneer a trail through the treacherous Khumbu Icefall, which starts at about 19,800 feet. The Americans were Willi Unsoeld, Jim Whittaker, and Lute Jerstad. The work was dangerous and exhausting, for the glacial movement and avalances of recent years had transformed the face of the icefall into a wild, slanting chaos of cliffs and chasms. If the advance task force could have avoided the icefall, they would have. Unfortunately it represented the sole entrance to the Western Cwm. Once the floor of the Cwm was reached, the Americans would get a crack at scaling the summit of Everest. It was the icefall or nothing.

The five climbers groped and hacked and twisted their way higher and higher through a labyrinth of snow and ice. Once they reached the icefall opening their pace slackened considerably, for the route was a shambles of broken blocks and grinding ice, with knee-deep snow in places and jumbled masses of rubble to crawl over. Lute's diary refers to the experience as "spine-tingling." Progress was slow, but they worked doggedly, chopping out hundreds of steps in the ice, and installing ropes and ladders so the Sherpas could pass through with their heavy loads on the way to stocking the advance camps that would be built later. It was not a job for the weak-hearted, building that trail across the icefall, because there was menace above them in the prospect of collapsing ice, and menace below them in the snow-hidden crevasses. Some of the ice blocks were double and triple the size of freight cars, forcing the climbers to detour and backtrack and zigzag to get around them. The only successful route through the icefall would require covering five times the airline distance and several days' time, but there was no other choice. To make matters worse, the temperature inside the icefall itself was like an oven, about 90 degrees, and the sweat poured off the faces of the climbers, soaking their clothing. They plodded on, and by mid-afternoon had finished marking a route nearly two thirds of the way through the hardest part of the icefall. They were well ahead of their timetable and toyed with the idea of going all the way to the top, but gave it up because of fatigue. It also would have meant coming back down in darkness, and none of the men wanted to risk the return trip to Base Camp at night.

They arrived at Base Camp at 3:15 P.M., dehydrated and dead tired, but happy. Lute drank three quarts of fruit juices at one sitting that evening to replace the body liquid he had lost. Even then it was not necessary to answer a nature call.

In mountaineering, no two days are alike. Sometimes a day that begins calmly will end with the most terrible events. The following day, March 23, was destined to be just such a day.

Early that morning, Jake Breitenbach, Dick Pownall, Gil Roberts, and two Sherpas, Ang Pema

and Ila Tsering, left Base Camp and headed up
through the icefall to finish chopping out the trail
that Jerstad, Whittaker, Unsoeld, and their two
Sherpas had worked on the previous day.

Dick Pownall was in the lead, Ang Pema was
behind him, and Jake Breitenbach was on the rear of
the first rope. Ila Tsering and Gil Roberts shared the
second rope. When more than three men go on such
a mission, it is customary for the party to be split up
into ropes of two or three each. They may spread out
over the trail in parallel routes to save time and
lessen the danger of dislodged falling particles, or
they may follow the first rope in tandem and call for
a lifeline over the difficult pitches. On the gentler
slopes of a glacier and on snow that is soft enough for
kicking steps, the whole party often moves simul-
taneously. When anyone slips, the others drive the
point or blade of the ice ax into the snow and ride
the fall to a stop.

Five hours after starting out from Base Camp,
Dick Pownall reached the base of a giant ice cliff
and paused to catch his breath. Up to that point
there had been no serious trouble, but suddenly
there was a shattering explosion high above, and an
instant later the entire upper half of the 40-foot-high
wall of ice came crashing down. It was a cave-in such
as few mountaineers witness. The roar was deafening.

There was no time to yell. There was not even
time to think.

Thousands of tons of ice and snow peeled loose from the mountain—hanging chunks of ice as big as houses—and plunged and echoed down in the path of the startled climbers with paralyzing abruptness.

The ground beneath began to move and slide, and Pownall had no time even to recoil. He hadn't taken two steps before a mass of falling ice and snow hit, almost smothering the life out of him. Directly in the way of the maëlstrom was Jake, and he was buried in an instant. Luck was with Gil Roberts— saved by a providential delay when he paused briefly to clean his glasses. Otherwise he would have been standing alongside Jake when the ice fell. As it was he was thrown backward by the sheer force of the blow.

Then all was still.

Finally, life stirred again. Gil sat up. There was a killing pain around his ribs and he rubbed his head gingerly, trying to remember where he was and how he got there. He should have been dead, according to the rules. And Jake? He was dead—he *had* to be dead—because the last thing Gil remembered was seeing those tons of frozen missiles plummeting on top of poor Jake, burying him in darkness and oblivion. Yet falling ice is unpredictable. It often plays weird tricks. Like leaving Gil alive when he should have been dead. And perhaps, Jake, Ang Pema, and Pownall, too. . . . Ila Tsering? He had been standing just clear of the target area and miraculously was unhurt. Gil got to his feet. "Come on, Ila, dig!" he shouted. Feverishly they worked. Then, wild-eyed, Tsering caught at Gil's sleeve. "There, Sahib, there! Him!" The limp figure of Dick Pownall was trapped underneath a half-ton block of ice. He was being slowly crushed to death. But he moved and groaned. He was still alive.

"Chop, Ila, chop!" cried Gil. The two men hacked away at that ice chunk for fully ten minutes, splitting it in half and gradually easing the weight from Dick's chest and wresting him from death's grip.

The hectic search continued. They found Ang Pema draped upside down under another huge ice block, squirming and turning blue. The side of his face was tipped with pink where the edges of the ice had gashed him. Looking up at Gil, the injured Sherpa sobbed, "Ang Pema finished, Sahib . . . Ang Pema finished."

"Take it easy," Gil soothed. "We're going to get you out."

Luck was with Ang Pema, too. He was close to death, but breathing.

Slowly, oh, so slowly, it seemed, they worked with ice axes cutting the stunned Sherpa free. So close, so close. A few more minutes and he would be a statistic of the expedition. Inches grew and spread. He was being extracted from a hole less than a foot in diameter. They could get their arms around the heavy buttocks now, they could lift and haul beneath the shoulders, they could exert more of their own weight. *Easy.* They had him up, riding on their straining arms.

And Jake? There was no sign of life where only minutes before he had been standing. There was only the icy calmness. Obviously he had met instant death. Now his body was permanently entombed far back under the ice wall—a victim of Everest's wrath. Resignedly, Gil and Ila lifted the bleeding and dazed Pownall and Ang Pema to their feet, and started crutching them back down to Base Camp.

Down at headquarters, meanwhile, the shouts and confusion up on the icefall had brought men charging out of their tents. Jimmy Roberts was staring intently through binoculars.

"Something's terribly wrong up there," he said, holding the glasses to his eyes. Then everyone was speaking at once. "I see a lot of milling around but only four men standing." "Where's the other man?" "They're starting to come down." "Who's missing?"

Sure enough, there were only four men coming down. Two of them appeared to be hurt; stumbling, now sitting down, now getting up again, and blundering erratically on again. "Get them on the radio!" somebody cried. But radio contact was impossible. Their radio was not working. The reason for its failure was painfully clear. Jake had been carrying the walkie-talkie. He was the one, then, who was

missing. "Let's get up there!" Barry Bishop shouted.
Base Camp was immediately transformed into an
emergency rescue area.

Hurrying to the scene were Lute, Willi Unsoeld, Jim Whittaker, Dave Dingman, Jimmy Roberts, Barry Bishop, Nawang Gombu, and Girmi
Dorje. Climbing at superhuman speed, the rescue
party caught up to the injured men about 400 feet
below the spot of the accident. Ice, snow, tattered
clothing, blotches of blood, glaring sun, the smell
of disinfectants, Ang Pema's sobbing—it all swam
past them. They were beside the injured men now,
and in the next instant, in what seemed like a long
obstacle race downhill, most of the rescuers and the
injured were moving as a coordinated team, crouch-
ing and hauling together, Ang Pema's head dripping
crimson and hanging foolishly, his mouth making
strange jabberings.

While the others went back to camp, Lute and
Whittaker and Willi Unsoeld continued on up the
icefall. They knew they had to make one last effort
to recover Jake's body.

The search proved fruitless. There was no trace
of their fallen comrade. Finally, at 8 o'clock, under
the light of the moon, they slogged back down to
Base Camp, tired, beaten, their spirits plunged into
black despair.

If Lute Jerstad lives to be a very old man he
will not forget the somber scene he witnessed in

passing Jake's tent upon his return to camp from above. Inside, stretched out on Jake's sleeping bag in the dark, was Nima Tensing, who had been personal Sherpa for both Lute and Jake. Nima was a stocky, tough-looking, yet sensitive little man, with an ugly scar over one eye. But when he smiled—and he smiled often—all that he was inside opened up, and his decency and his innate kindness reached out like a soft hand to touch those around him. Nima was lying there, quietly intense, establishing communion with the image of his lost sahib. He had not gone to Jake's tent that morning and said good-by to him, wishing him Godspeed. He was ashamed of the oversight and was taking it out on himself. It was bad to have Jake go like that, without so much as a parting handshake. Nima had grown very fond of Jake in the few short weeks they had been together, and his death seemed vicious and something that should not have been.

Late that night, Lute got out his diary and wrote:

March 23—At 2:00 P.M. today Jake was killed when an entire ice wall collapsed on top of him at about 19,000 feet. Pownall was injured and badly shaken, and Ang Pema was very near death, buried head down in ice blocks. Gil and Tsering got them out. . . . Unsoeld, Whittaker, and I later went back up to the scene of the accident to make certain Jake was really dead—and we cried all the way up there. We could not find him, for he was buried under an ice wall 40 feet high, 20 feet wide, and 60 feet long. How absurd is man in the face of nature—like ants chewing on the leaves of eternity. It was purely an act of God. There was no carelessness. The chances of such accidents happening are about the same as of a train hitting an automobile: the car must be there at the exact instant the train crosses the road. Jake was there at that precise flick of the eyelash. We are all stunned by this thing, but we will bounce back. Jake would want us to. The fact that we will push on probably sounds cruel but Jake understands. He knows you don't stop driving a car because a friend is killed in one. He was one of those rare people who truly enjoyed the life he lived—who knew himself and followed his ambition. We shall all miss Jake. *God bless you, Jake, on your new journey.*

8

The Impatient Days of Trial

Men of action do not dwell on death. They accept it and go on. Except for a brief inquest on March 24, the case was closed. Dyhrenfurth regrouped his forces without delay, and the work was resumed. They plunged into the strenuous task of unpacking food and equipment, securing tents and supplies, and put in motion all the numerous little routines that demanded attention preparatory to the ascent of the summit itself. Hours were spent poring over maps and charts and studying the heights above them through telescope and binoculars. Soon now they would begin to establish a series of six advance camps on the South Col route, starting at 20,200 feet and extending all the way up to 27,450 feet. The gravity of the immense maneuver is reflected in Jerstad's diary:

All of us know we are stepping into a world of the unknown, of the misery of high altitude, of heat and cold, and of men living at close quarters for months at a time. We are prepared to face these obstacles, for all of us have been on expeditions before and are trained and conditioned to meet them. We realize that we are pitted against an enemy which never relaxes its guard and is always conjuring up new and more horrendous trials. Personally I know there are going to be moments when I will want to quit, when the odds will seem too great. I also know that I cannot quit. I owe it to my teammates to go on. If I should let down even for a minute, someone else might die —and we have already lost one man! It would be so easy to quit, and difficult to spur others on, but each of us has silently vowed to carry the ball if someone fumbles it, and to do our very best to get the fallen man up and going again.

Within just a matter of a few days Base Camp resembled a tent city, with scores of tents anchored in the snow and filled to overflowing with such essentials of survival as 216 cylinders of oxygen, hundreds of waterproof cartons stocked with food supplies, 2 miles of nylon rope and many trunks of scientific gear.

Subzero temperatures posed many problems now and added to the daily struggle. On cold nights the mercury dipped 16 degrees below zero, freezing some of the equipment—their portable tape recorders, for example—so solidly it had to be thawed out before the men could use it. Jerstad wrote in his diary that the cold air was bothering him more than the elevation. "It's even getting too cold for nature calls at night," he noted. "We have plastic urinals that work fine until one of us upsets one in our sleep and then—well!"

The scientific aspects of the assault on Everest started to move into high gear with the establishment of Base Camp. Dr. Jim Lester went from American to American, collecting their dreams and studying the effects of high altitude on their thoughts and emotions. "Lester says there are quite a few dreams about redhaired women!" wrote Lute. "I don't know what significance can be attached to that." Dr. Dick Emerson, the sociologist, had the Americans keeping special diaries as part of his study to determine how they got along with each other under growing stress and strain. And Dr. Will Siri continued his physiological experiments with tests such as having each man step up and down on a box for three minutes at a time to measure changes in blood pressure and respiration. It was an agonizing

75

ordeal at 17,800 feet, but everyone took it in stride and with few complaints. Dr. Siri also collected frequent samples of blood and urine.

Lute wrote:

When he begins playing with blood we all cringe. Thoughts of the needle are not popular up here. Whittaker and I were gathering urine samples today for Siri and the Sherpas suspected we had really cracked up. I can imagine them saying to each other: "With all the outdoors up here—and the stupid sahibs collect urine in bottles!"

The hours hurried along. All sorts of tasks, small and large, occupied the men's time. They didn't rush them. Life in the high Himalayas had already taught them patience. They had recognized from the beginning that an orderly routine was the only defense against brain-cracking loneliness. And they often had to admit to themselves that they were lonely. Try as they might, they could not accept their loneliness casually; it was too big, too real, especially in the unnatural blue and inky black of night. So in an effort not to dwell on it they tried to keep their days crowded with systematic duties. The revised timetable called for the completion of Camp 1 by March 31. A decision was made to establish it at the lower end of the Cwm at 20,200 feet. Some 1,100 feet higher, in a long snow valley directly under Everest's southwest flank, Camp 2, or what would otherwise be known as Advance Base Camp, would be set up. The work promised to be less difficult up there where the snow was smooth and the slope gentle.

The day-to-day entries in Lute's diary give a graphic picture of the following weeks of struggle leading up to Zero Hour, when the first climbing party would make the assault on the summit itself.

March 25—We are going to split up into two teams. One team will travel along the familiar route toward the Lhotse Face and the South Col, and the other team will reconnoiter the possibilities of a new route over on the unclimbed West Ridge. Unsoeld, Bishop, Hornbein, Emerson, Corbet, and Dingman will make up the West Ridge team. The Lhotse Face team will consist of Dyhrenfurth, Siri, Whittaker, Pownall, Auten, Roberts, and myself. The rest of the guys are mostly specialists in science, communications, and photography and will stay in the vicinity of Advance Base, joining us only at such times and places as they are needed and as is possible. At this stage the West Ridge venture is only a *reconnaissance,* but it may grow to a full-sized assault if it looks feasible.... It's considerably cooler tonight, down around zero. Unsoeld, Whittaker, and I are getting up early in the morning to see if we can bang our way from Base Camp clear into the Cwm; several of the other guys will spend the day improving the route from the dump until their energy runs out. ... The tragic news of Jake's death should just about be hitting the streets back in America today. I'm wondering how my folks will feel now about my being up here.

March 27—Whittaker, Unsoeld, Gombu, and I worked for 11 hours today—and an 11-hour Himalayan day is a long one! Our objective was to push the

MOUNT EVEREST
29,028 FT.

South Summit
28,750

Northeast Ridge

Yellow Band

Camp 6
27,450

South Col

Camp 5 West
27,250

Camp 5
26,200

West Ridge

CHANGTSE
24,780

Camp 4 West
25,100

Camp 3 West
23,800

Western

Camp 2
21,350

Lho La Pass

Camp 1
20,200

PUMORI
23,442

Khumbu Icefall

Base Camp
17,800

Khumbu Glacier

©FPC

78

LHOTSE
27,923

Yellow Band
Lhotse Face
Geneva
Spur
Camp 4
24,900

NUPTSE
25,726

Cwm

Camp
3
22,900

BARUNTSE
23,688

79

route all the way to the Cwm. We left Base at 7:30 and arrived at the dump in 1 hour, 53 minutes. That's really hoofing when we are not fully acclimatized. We paused only long enough for hot coffee. After fairly stiff going, we reached the last great wall at noon—60 feet of vertical ice. The safest way was to climb over it. Unsoeld and Whittaker went first. Jim put in three ice screws before Willi relieved him. I belayed Willi and was supposed to work next, but he got into a couple of spots where it was easier to go up than down, so he continued for two hours at 20,000 feet! The wall was finally negotiated after three hours. Willi put up a fixed rope for me and I crawled up. We moved on into the Cwm until we reached about 20,300 feet, where we spotted a giant crevasse. At 4 P. M. we turned around and came back down to Base Camp, arriving at 6:30. None of us are fully acclimatized, and we are pretty tired tonight. I have to admire both Unsoeld and Whittaker. I wonder if I could have mustered the strength they did to manage such vigorous ice-climbing after such a tough day and in thin air. What powerful men! I was very impressed, if not a bit humble, after watching their performance.

March 28—Corbet, Bishop, and Hornbein took two Sherpas and went to stay up at the dump today. The wind blew and whistled fiercely all night and they were late getting started. They left Base at 10 A.M. and now are below the wall getting ready to put up four sections of aluminum ladder bolted together from a block to the ice wall. They'll chop big steps into the other portion and put up fixed ropes. Camp 1 will be established in the Cwm at about 20,300 feet. . . . After yesterday's long day, Unsoeld, Whittaker, and I are taking it easy. Gil Roberts, Dingman, Prather, and Emerson and 20 Sherpas will occupy Camp 1 tomorrow. They'll also begin exploring a route to Camp 2 (Advance Base), to be established at 21,350 feet. It's just a long slog between camps. Fourteen extra icefall Sherpas reported here tonight to begin relaying loads tomorrow. We hope to get in a good enough route so that they can carry all the way from Base to Camp 1 and return to Base. It will cut down logistic problems if that can be done. . . . My weight is down 15 pounds to 141. I hope I don't lose any more, because I'm going to need all the strength I can get. . . . I've just finished packing my gear for a trip to Advance Base. I doubt if Whittaker, Unsoeld, and I will be finding the route between Camps 1 and 2, but will move to Camp 2 and reconnoiter the Lhotse Face while the West Ridge is being explored.

March 29—We're still lolling around in the sunshine here at Base. Whittaker and I spent part of the day unpacking the oxygen bottles remaining here —182 of them. . . . Another lift of 20 loads was made to the dump today. Bishop, Corbet, and Hornbein reported the route to the Cwm to be in excellent condition now and fit for the Sherpas to carry loads over.

March 30—Whittaker, Prather, and Gil Roberts went up to occupy Camp 1 today. Two Sherpas went with them. Tomorrow they'll push the route to the Cwm. Twelve Sherpas carried light loads from here and picked up Camp 1 gear at the dump and carried it to the top of the icefall. They made the carry in four hours, which speaks well for the route. . . . Our extra icefall Sherpas sure are tough-looking blokes. They wear any kind of boots, pants, shirts, etc., and carry loads in rustic baskets or right on their backs. I don't think I'd want to get into an argument with any of them. . . . We have so much equipment here now that I'm leaving a lot of stuff behind when we move up. We have three sets of Duofold underwear, down underwear, and down pants. I'll solve my laundry problem by wearing my Duofold underwear until it is grimy—and then throw it away! The Sherpas now have our kitchen organized. It looks like a supermarket. . . .

The little war against the big mountain was 38 days old by now. Boredom, sweat, a never-ending succession of problems—the physical pressures were starting to show. The men were thinned down to bone and muscle, sometimes edgy, sometimes griping or silent. Their faces were drawn with monotony, their minds seared raw with it. For the first time, Lute's diary hints of open rebellion within the American ranks:

We witnessed several blowups tonight. First, the Sherpas demanded inner sleeping bags. Since we have none for them here we will have to have them brought up from Namche Bazar. It was a rather silly argument, but it is all settled and there are no hard feelings. A second blowup came in our own ranks when Siri asked that a doctor here assist him in his iron studies. Gil and Will exchanged a few harsh words and then Norman Dyhrenfurth entered with others into the fray and it got quite noisy. The up-shot of it all is that Dave Dingman will stay at Base for the next five days. Whittaker has replaced him on the Camp 1 team.

March 31—My departure has been delayed a day. Pownall and I will go up to Camp 1 tomorrow, and to Camp 2 the next day to work on the Lhotse Face. Unsoeld, Hornbein, and Emerson moved up to Camp 1 today, while Whittaker and crew made a round trip from Camp 1 to Camp 2 and back again. On the way to Camp 1 Hornbein suffered pains in his stomach and stayed at the dump, but he is okay now. . . . Speaking of sickness, we received a note from Sir Edmund Hillary, who's leading a minor expedition down below, asking for smallpox vaccine. Evidently there is a serious epidemic down there. . . . The weather is growing colder daily. Clear but cold. I have let my hair grow long, for it comes down around my neck and keeps me warm. My cheeks are blistered, and my nose is red and bulbous from the wind. But how I look is immaterial; what is impor-tant is how I feel. And except for a slight cold my health is sound. We have little to fear up here from disease, for Everest's refrigerating temperatures make it a sterile world. The only germs are those we have brought with us.

April 1—April Fool's Day—and it is no joke. Bishop, Pownall, and I hiked up to Camp 1 here today. We sent our duffels ahead and carried our personal gear. I somehow got all fouled up and ended up carrying 60 pounds; nearly drove me into the ground. It was a slow, five-hour trip. We stopped for an hour at the dump and rested. No one here at Camp 1 went on up to Camp 2 today because it snowed. Unsoeld, Emerson, Whittaker, Hornbein, Gil Roberts, Bishop, Pownall, and I are all staying here tonight. Our Sherpas came with us and put up our tents, unpacked our bags, blew up our air mattresses, and set out books, lights, etc., for us. It was snowing all the while, too. We then sat six in a tent and talked. Whittaker contacted Base on radio and Al Auten put us through to Katmandu; spoke with them for 15 minutes, making us feel less remote way up here. We then ate in the 10-by-10-foot Sherpa tent. Right now avalanches are pouring off the West Ridge and Nuptse—they're keeping me awake! But we are on a crevasse ledge and very safe. Above the roar of the avalanches I can hear Willi playing his harmonica in the next tent. What a contrast in sounds.

April 2, Camp 2—Advance Base. Unsoeld, Bishop, Whittaker, and I left Camp 1 for here at 11 A.M. After some argument about the weights of their packs, 10 Sherpas carried for us. We were all carrying over 50 pounds; I had 60 pounds and Unsoeld probably had more than that. Gombu also carried up and is staying with us. We really were dragging. I felt weaker on this trip than ever before. To never have been over 21,000 feet before and then carry a 60-pound pack to 21,500 feet, is downright ridiculous. We were all beginning to wonder if we would make it. I was carrying an uncomfortable pack, and I have seldom been in more agony, caused by inefficient equipment and tired, bursting lungs. I tried to think of home, sunshine—anything—to take my mind off my misery. But I'll get used to this altitude and will look back at my weakness and foolishness with a smile—maybe.

84

April 3—Whittaker, Gombu, and I put in the route to Camp 3 today. It took us three and a half hours from Camp 2. The wind was blowing snow around, and it was very cold—9 degrees above zero. About noon the weather warmed up a little, and the sun came out for a while. The route to Camp 3 is slowly uphill until the last 400 or 500 feet. Camp 3 is the same site as the Indian expedition's Camp 4 (22,900 feet). I felt remarkably good after yesterday's horrible struggle. Whittaker carried a light pack. I didn't carry anything, so I broke trail all the way up. I feel I got the easy end of the deal, for there was little step-chopping or deep snow. Meanwhile, over on the West Ridge, Bishop and Unsoeld blazed through the hard part of the route to about 23,000 feet. . . . Hornbein, Emerson, Gil Roberts, and Pownall came up here with a Sherpa carry today—but still not a heavy one. They are as tired as we were yesterday. . . . Gombu was feeling ill today—stomach trouble and diarrhea. It slowed him down considerably.

April 4, Camp 2—We all took the day off to write letters, read, and rest. We also went over the logistics again for both routes and discovered how woefully short we are on loads up here. . . . Barry Corbet, Dingman, and Dyhrenfurth came up from Camp 1 today; Norman will spend the night here and then go down tomorrow. Two Sherpas also came up to stay. Corbet and Dingman carried up Jim's and my duffels, an extremely nice gesture, and then went down again. Tomorrow Jim, Gombu, Pownall, and I will carry light loads to Camp 3, and the next day Jim and Gombu will probably work up to Camp 4 while Pownall and I move up to occupy Camp 3, then continue to Camp 4 the day after that. Whittaker and I would like to work together but Jim will go with Gombu. Pownall is a rock man and uneasy on ice, but a great climber. This evening we are going to record a tape on our little portable tape machine which will be for a benefit back at Katmandu for the burned woman's hospital bill. She will be out of the hospital in a week.

April 5, Camp 2—Whittaker, Pownall, Gombu, Gil Roberts, and I began ferrying loads to establish Camp 3. Gil got ill and stayed at about 22,330 while we went on. We set up a four-man tent at what our altimeter indicated was 23,200 feet. We were really getting tired carrying 40 pounds apiece at 23,000 feet without oxygen. Even Gombu was tired. . . . Bishop and Hornbein struck out for the top of the West Shoulder at 24,200 feet, and came within about 400 feet of it. They saw no great obstacles beyond where they turned back. . . . Unsoeld and Emerson set out to improve the route to the dump, but Dick became sick and they turned back. Ultimately Dick went down to Camp 1 with the Sherpas, and Willi took Nima Dorje up to the dump to work on the route. When we returned from Camp 3 there were nine Sherpas here ready to spend the night.

April 6—This morning we were roused from our bags by a radio message saying that Maynard Miller had broken his foot at Base Camp. It turned out to be no emergency—we kept thinking of Jake at the icefall! Gil may go down to tend to it, since he has not as yet acclimatized very well to this altitude anyway. . . . Unsoeld left with nine Sherpas to carry to the West Ridge dump, located at about 22,500 feet. The rest of us just lolled around Camp 2 all day sorting our gear, resting, and discussing plans. . . . Eleven Sherpa loads came up, and Dingman arrived to replace Emerson on the West Ridge. Corbet also was ill, and both he and Emerson may go down to Base for rest. . . . Dan Doody got up to Camp 1 yesterday, and Al Auten was supposed to be there today. Will Siri and Jim Lester made a dash to the dump and down again, apparently almost ruining Lester. . . . Whittaker and Gombu will occupy Camp 3 tomorrow and work on the route to Camp 4. Pownall and I will move up on the 8th, and Jim and Gombu will return to Camp 2 to rest. We'll work on the route to Camp 4 and hope to get a tent and two Sherpa loads up. We want to go to 25,000 feet, fixing the traverse to the Col. We will return to Camp 2 on the 10th of April.

April 7, Camp 2—There's not much action around here today. Dingman isn't feeling well and he and Unsoeld are spending the day with us. However, Bishop, Hornbein, and seven heavily loaded Sherpas left for the dump to spend the night, and tomorrow they will move camp to the crest of the West Ridge at over 24,000 feet. On the South Col route, Whittaker and Gombu took along two Sherpas, Nima Dorje and Ang Nuru, to Camp 3 and sent them back. It started to snow terribly, but Jim and Gombu and all the West Ridge bunch kept working. . . . Pownall and I cleaned up the cook's kitchen and washed all the dishes; I've felt weak and listless all day, the result of inactivity. A Sherpa carry involving 11 Sherpas from Camp 1 came up at 1 o'clock. There were no sahibs with them. I guess Corbet is still recovering, and Emerson is back at Base. Apparently Maynard's foot is not broken after all, but badly

bruised, and no doctor will have to go down to him.
. . . The weather has been cloudy today, though the
sun is trying to peek through. It looks as though it
might clear up. We've been very lucky where the
weather is concerned, so can't complain about one
small squall—but I pray that's all it is.

April 8, Camp 3—Whittaker and Gombu had a lot
of trouble getting onto the first rise above Camp 3. It
took about three hours. They spent a lot of time fixing the route and finding one. About 1 o'clock they
reached somewhere around 24,000 feet and turned
back. The wind was blowing quite hard, and they
fouled themselves up trying to take a different route
down. The West Shoulder team didn't budge from
camp; it was too stormy. They sent six Sherpas down
to Camp 2, and they'll carry straight through to the
Shoulder tomorrow. . . . Pownall and I went from
Camp 2 to Camp 3 in two and three quarters hours
with light packs; two Sherpas carried loads. Now
Dick and I are trying to figure out how to sleep with
oxygen—our first time. Tomorrow we will climb on
3 liters [1 liter equals about 1.0567 U.S. quarts] to
Camp 4 and work down on less or no oxygen. This
is the highest either of us has ever slept.

April 9, Camp 2—Dick Pownall and I started out
with oxygen from Camp 3 at 8:30 A.M. We spent
almost two hours getting up the first shelf of the
Lhotse Face. We traveled on 3 liters' flow for three
hours and suddenly discovered that Dick's tank or
regulator was leaking. We cut back to 2 liters, and
then to 1. At 1 P.M. he had only 50 liters left and
we were at the spot where Whittaker and Gombu
turned back. We continued up a rise toward ice walls
and found two fixed ropes left over from the Indian

expedition. We were at about 24,300 feet, and by this time Dick had only 30 liters left. We started back down at 2 o'clock without oxygen, and it sure made a difference in our breathing. About halfway down we turned it on again to get up a slight slope and down a fixed rope. Just as we reached the tent at Camp 3, Dick's bottle gave out completely. . . . We brewed up some hot tea and food, and after eating we came back down here to Camp 2. It is much warmer here than at Camp 3. Our mail and a hot meal were waiting for us here. I read letters for an hour and finally went to sleep with a smile.

April 10, Camp 2—Everest is growing impatient with us. We know the day is not far away when the monsoon will hit, and then all hope of mass success will be gone. This means striking hard and striking fast in the time still left. Whittaker, Corbet, and I carried to Camp 3 today, dumped our small loads, and found a new route above Camp 3 which will save at least one and a half hours to Camp 4. It was extremely hot on the way to Camp 3, but when we began working on the face it snowed. We went to about 23,300 feet and then came back down. It was cold and blowing all the way back to Camp 2.

April 11, Camp 2—I didn't do much of anything today except prepare loads for the Sherpas going to Camp 3. Twenty-two oxygen bottles went up to Camp 3 today. That camp is slowly getting stocked. Norman has picked the first four-man assault squad for the summit: Whittaker, Gombu, Pownall, and I are it! I hope it doesn't change. We still think we can get on top by May Day. I hope we can flood the summit with climbers and then go home.

April 12, Camp 2—In several days Pownall and I will lead a carry to Camp 4. We'll stay there and put up fixed ropes to the Geneva Spur. At noon today Whittaker and Gombu went up to occupy Camp 3; tomorrow they'll take two Sherpas to Camp 4 with tent, fixed ropes, etc. We're getting high on the mountain now. Pownall and I will move up to occupy Camp 3 tomorrow. We hope to get a full carry of at least eight Sherpas to Camp 4 the next day. They'll presumably go empty from Camp 2 to Camp 3 and pick up loads there to carry to Camp 4. . . . Jim Lester came up to Camp 2 today. He looked good and felt all right, but he was tired. I hadn't seen him for about two weeks. . . . We expect the members of the West Ridge reconnaissance team to be down at any moment. They have been spending the entire day exploring up there. . . . Dan Doody showed me some things about the summit movie camera today. Pownall and I will take it up to Camp 4 with us.

April 13—Today Whittaker, Gombu, and the two Sherpas left Camp 3 at 7 A.M. and established Camp 4 at 24,900 feet, high on Everest's Lhotse Face. It took them four and a half hours. They put up a tent and left a sleeping bag in it. The West Ridge gang came down tonight and two of them (Hornbein and Unsoeld) are hot to go right back, but Bishop and Dingman want to go on the Col route. The West Ridge will go ahead slowly as the big push is for the Col in the next 10 days. This has stirred up some heated discussions and hurt feelings among the pro-West Ridgers. Unsoeld and Hornbein both feel they have been sold out for a mass attempt on the Col route.

April 14, Camp 3—Pownall and I came to Camp 3 with seven Sherpas on schedule today. They moved their personal gear up here to live. Their job will be to stock Camp 4 and ultimately the Col. Tomorrow we will move with two Sherpas to Camp 4 and spend the night, attempting to reach the Col the following day. We will put in a fixed rope across the Yellow Band near Camp 4. At 3 o'clock this afternoon it began snowing and hasn't stopped. Dick and I are sharing a two-man tent; the seven Sherpas are in two four-man tents. Auten and Gil Roberts went up above here today and chopped steps in the route's first bad spot and came down in the snow. The Sherpas had tea waiting for them here. Only about 15 more days and we'll have this old mountain licked —if the weather holds out. Gombu is very happy now that the big day draws near. He said he has never seen climbing to match our performance. He is practically one of us now and is delighted to be part of the first assault team.

There actually were two wars going on up there on Everest. There was the war of logistics and maps. Then there was the war of homesick, weary, dedicated, persevering men who went without baths, oxygen, indoor plumbing, all the comforts of home; uncompromising men who were anxious to get to the top; tenacious men who lugged themselves, their spirits, and their loads along a rugged route and did it with humor and dignity and courage. That was Lute Jerstad's Everest. But he did not climb in fear. He had had some close shaves, but had escaped injury; and when a professional climber goes a long time, as Lute had done, with danger all around him, without ever getting so much as a scratch, he sometimes builds up a feeling of indestructibility about himself. He doesn't worry too much about what might happen.

Lute no longer questioned Everest as a place of evil reputation. He already had written it into his personal records as the bloody arena that had swallowed up one American, and the cruelest phase of the battle was still to be fought. Almost daily now Everest intensified its pressure. The wind bit deep. Snow piled up in icy drifts. The oxygenless heights pinched the climbers' lungs. More and more of them were fading into gaunt, beaten caricatures of the men who had left the United States physically fit. Lute laments in his diary:

I'm down to 140 pounds. The food is quite unpalatable at times. Dick Emerson is also having trouble keeping it down. Gil Roberts isn't well, and Dan Doody is positively shot. Dan tried hiking to Camp 3 and had to quit at 22,200 feet. Dr. Will Siri has been giving us a series of exercise tests to determine fluctuating pulse rate and blood pressure. These tests have revealed that we can hold our breath for only 12 seconds at this elevation. It feels awful. It feels as if all the years of strength and endurance are being drained into a thimble.

The struggle went on. At Camp 4, on April 15, Lute wrote:

Pownall and I and several Sherpas came up to Camp 4 today. One Sherpa got ill and stayed below. It snowed all night and during the day, forcing us to cut hundreds of new steps in the route. The weather cleared by the time we arrived here. I shot 150 feet of film today with the summit camera. Pownall's feet were very cold when we got here. I rubbed them, and he breathed oxygen for a while and is better now. The Sherpas think the route between Camps 3 and 4 is okay, although a bit long (2,000 feet). Tashi, who is 56 years old, told me: "This good route. You make good. This no monkey route. Monkey route no fixed ropes, no chopped steps. You make good route."

April 16, Camp 2—This has been a busy day. Pownall and I left Camp 4 at 10:30 A.M. for the South Col. We purposely started late, because we had been concerned about leaving before the sun came out; our boots were still wet from yesterday, and we were worried about frostbite. The Sherpas packed a tent, 15-pound stove, cook kit, cups, and some film and went with us. Dick and I carried fixed ropes, screws, rappel pickets, and oxygen bottles, about 40 pounds apiece. We reached the Yellow Band at about 25,000 feet at 11 A.M. It was covered with a foot of snow and sheer water ice, making it hard and slippery. We installed an anchor for a fixed rope, and I began chopping bucket steps across. The ice was so hard that I couldn't even get a screw or picket into it, so I just kept chopping and dragging the 200-foot fixed line with me. When it came to the end, we got three turns around a rock and anchored it. The next stages of the operation were similar: dragging fixed line and hoping to find a spot to anchor it. We got a small picket halfway in and used it. Then we ran out our 450 feet of rope all tied together, but we couldn't find a place to anchor it.

Dick went out ahead of where the rope would reach and discovered that he could drive in a 4-foot picket; there was nothing to do but use it. Our fixed Manila rope wouldn't reach, so we cut our climbing rope in half and tied it on. It took us two hours to complete the task—and we had figured on only a half hour! By this time it was 1 P.M. and the clouds were rolling in. We debated whether to push on. We knew we could spend another day at Camp 4, so we went on. We crossed another gully to the Geneva Spur, scrambling over rocks. The Sherpas cut off below us, taking a route we hadn't known about. At 3 P.M. we came out on top of a snow dome looking into the South Col. We waited there wondering where the Sherpas were. Suddenly they popped into view about 300 feet below us, entering the Col. We were quite high, higher than necessary, at about 26,400 feet. We met the Sherpas at the Col with their loads and picked out a tent site. The South Col has been called the highest junkyard in the world, with oxygen bottles, masks, tattered tents, clothing, cookery, etc., scattered all over the place. Chotari [a Sherpa] dug through one of the old Indian tents and found three pairs of perfectly good heavy socks. . . . The wind picked up and really roared. We went back down via the new Sherpa route. It juts out only about 50 feet, while the old route mounts 200 feet and is difficult to get out of. We left at 4 P.M. and were back at Camp 4 at 5:15. We packed up our gear there and continued coming down. I made radio contact at 6 P.M. and told Camp 2 we'd come all the way down. We arrived at Camp 3 in darkness and instructed Chotari and Nima Tensing to spend the night there; they were really beat, for they hadn't been using oxygen. Pownall and I plowed out into the darkness toward Camp 2, using our head lamps over the crevasses. Despite the long, hard day, we were in good spirits. We sang and talked most of the way, the stars were out and it was beautiful. I even recited some poetry until I ran out of breath. We hit camp here at 9:15 P.M., ate a good supper, talked to Jim, Willi, and Tom, then went to bed at 10 P.M.

April 17, Camp 2—I'm spending the day resting after yesterday's Col trip. I feel good, and except for a sore calf there are no aftereffects. Chotari and Nima Tensing came down from Camp 3 to rest, but already Chotari wants to go back up to the Col. Unfortunately we miscalculated the logistics, and the mistake will set us back several days. We need 38 loads on the Col for the two four-man assaults; also, in our absence, the assault teams have been changed. It was felt that the original first team of Whittaker, Gombu, Pownall, and myself was putting all the eggs in one basket, so Pownall and I were put on the second team. As it stands now, Whittaker and Gombu will be with Dyhrenfurth and Ang Dawa, and Dick and I will be accompanied by Barry Bishop and Girmi Dorje. Norman doesn't particularly want to go, but with Dan Doody, our professional cameraman, knocked out by thrombophlebitis, there's no other alternative. The motion pictures can bring in a lot of money for future expeditions, and I am happy to step aside for that. Dick and I will still get our crack at the summit. Of course, Whittaker and I had hoped to be together going to the top, but the expedition comes first.

April 18, Camp 2—I've spent another day doing practically nothing. Several of us sat around talking

95

about home, our families, friends, being nostalgic. It showed us all wanting to get back to America as soon as this thing is climbed. We also got into an argument over the goraks, those big, black, disheveled and ugly birds that dwell around our camps. They're so awkward they have to take off downhill to fly. Where they sleep, or what they eat when no one is up here, no one seems to know; but their saw-edged beaks are tough enough to cut through heavy cardboard food boxes, and they'd be only too happy to share our tents with us. Those blasted birds wake us up at 5:30 A.M. pecking at our food boxes. They are not easily frightened. They resemble something Mickey Spillane created. What ugly things. When I see four of them in a cluster I usually work the other way! Most of the guys hate them, some of them like them. Dan Doody's feelings are somewhere in between. He says, "Here the goraks share the mountain with another group of misfits, oddballs, or whatever you want to call us." This reminds me of a thought I had the other day while Pownall and I were up at 26,000 feet. A blackbird or crow flew overhead and I thought to myself: "What a ridiculous place for a bird—on second thought, what a ridiculous place for people!"

April 19, Camp 2—More random observations while we're waiting around camp here for the signal to move up. The weather has turned cold and windy. Wind alone is no hardship, and neither is the freezing temperature, but a combination of the two is a quick killer. You seldom think of the temperature without thinking of the wind velocity; combined they constitute the chill factor. The ink in our pens turns to ice, forcing the writer to reheat the penpoint over a candle flame at the end of every sentence. The rules for survival must be treated with utmost respect up here. . . . We read and reread the Swiss accounts of Everest and Lhotse today. Whittaker and I still hope to stay on the Col after Everest and try Lhotse. . . . Ang Nuru was sent back down to Base Camp today with what Gil Roberts thinks is hookworm.

April 20, Camp 2—Today has been another bad one. Heavy winds and snow prevented the Sherpas from moving out of Camps 3 and 4. A carry of 6 went from here to Camp 3, and 12 came up from Camp 1. There was some real excitement here early this morning. A spectacular avalanche crashed down off the mountainside, and though we are fairly well protected, most of the Sherpas took off like banty roosters in all directions, thinking it was coming all the way across the valley floor. Dan Doody got the scare of his life. He is hard of hearing and nearly walked smack into the path of the avalanche before he looked up and saw it coming. . . . We figured logistics again today and estimate that with a break in the weather and no more delays, the first summit team can move out of here in five days. We will follow them the day after. We are impatient now to get the summit assault under way. It is difficult to sit around waiting.

April 21, Camp 2—We were very disappointed today as we watched through binoculars the first 7 Sherpas leave Camp 4 and turn back with their loads at the Yellow Band. They had spent two nights at 25,000 feet without oxygen, and the wind may have turned them back. We won't know the full reason until tomorrow when we move up to Camp 3. Chotari's party of 6 went up and occupied Camp 4 and should go on to the Col tomorrow. The Sherpas, incidentally, are involved in quite a hassle. It seems that of the 37 Sherpas we have with us, 4 of them are from Darjeeling. Two of the 4 now have a chance of going to the summit—Gombu and Ang Dawa. Girmi Dorje also has a chance, but he is from Solu Khumbu. This makes the ratio 2 to 1 in favor of Darjeeling, and the other Sherpas are beefing. Jimmy Roberts, who is in charge of the Sherpas, is hot under the collar, and he sent up a note yesterday explaining that Whittaker should have a Sherpa with him, Pownall should have one, Norman must have one, and I should have one. In other words, make sure that they're Solu Khumbus, not Darjeelings. If we did this, it would mean that each sahib would be accompanied by a Sherpa to the summit, almost as if we were being guided up. Well, we've objected. It isn't going to be that way. It would look bad if we didn't get to the top on our own; also we have spent $400,000 getting here, and we don't see any reason to pay the Sherpas and take them all to the summit, too. Gombu, from Darjeeling, has been singled out to go with Whittaker on the first attempt—and the Sherpa question ends there!

April 22, Camp 2—Today Chotari and 6 Sherpas went to the Col with loads, making us very happy. At the same time, 10 Sherpas left here for Camp 3 with the intention of carrying through to Camp 4 and the Col. With the magnificent way Jimmy Roberts has been juggling the Sherpas we should be able to get the first summit team on its way by the twenty-sixth. Summit days, barring bad weather, have been set for April 30 and May 1. The West Ridge attempt will be about eight days behind us—we hope. Pownall, Whittaker, and I went for a short two-hour hike to get some exercise this afternoon. We went up toward the West Ridge dump and got a different view of the Cwm. . . . Dan Doody's thrombosis has us all seriously worried. Gil Roberts has him on fluids and medication, hoping to dissolve the clot. We sure don't need an emergency at this crucial time. If the clot breaks, it can be fatal in the heart. Dan is getting a lot of praying from me.

April 23, Camp 2—Ten Sherpas went up to Camp 4 today despite the snow which fell most of the day, and Norman, Will Siri, Jimmy Roberts, Gombu, and seven Sherpas went from here to Camp 3. Meanwhile, over on the West Ridge, Unsoeld and Hornbein with four Sherpas carried to their dump. It snowed about three inches this afternoon, but Gombu has predicted seven days of good weather. That would give us just time enough for several summit assaults—we hope! The Sherpa weathermen are as reliable as the all-India forecasts. . . . Dan Doody is about the same; feels pretty good, he says, but still can't move, and Gil can't tell anything about the clot for at least another week. I have a stomachache today, which I hope is only from drinking too much coffee. At this stage of the battle— with our general deterioration and Doody's illness— I'm afraid I've become a bad case of paranoia.

April 24, Camp 2—We loafed around all morning but carried two food boxes toward Camp 3 this afternoon. It began snowing, and we met Gombu and Chotari coming down with a sick Sherpa who couldn't carry to Camp 4. We dropped the boxes on the flats about 500 feet below Camp 3 and returned here. I feel I'm getting very sick myself. I hope I have enough strength left to get up this mountain. I now have doubts about myself which I didn't have ten days ago. This is a hostile world. Very few men have ever really known it. I have the spreading suspicion that we don't belong up here, that outside our warm little tents the elements are king. Consequently we must be alert and on guard at all times, because it's fear and indecision and panic which kill you in the subzero world.

April 25, Camp 2—It snowed all day, and I doubt if the six Sherpas up at Camp 4 moved out of their tents. This will delay the summit assault one more day. It gets very discouraging. The low-pressure area just seems to hang over us and refuses to move. Maynard Miller says the barometer is rising, but still no change up here. . . . As for Doody, there's still no apparent change in his condition. The doctors won't know for several days. . . . We have merely laid around in our tents all day reading and writing letters. We are about out of fresh books up here. The weather had better clear soon, or we'll all have to go down to Base Camp and recuperate. We can't stand much more of this!

April 26, Camp 2—It snowed again all day long. Where's that good weather Gombu predicted? We still haven't heard from the Sherpas at Camp 4. I doubt if they could have carried to the Col. They might spend a third night up there, but then could be too weak to carry to the Col after three straight nights at an elevation just under 25,000 feet. At lunch today we had quite an irritable session over the Col versus West Ridge. Some heated words were thrown back and forth, causing hurt feelings on both sides. Hornbein was quite upset over it. . . . If the weather improves tomorrow, the first assault team will move out with 13 Sherpas. We'll follow with 8 Sherpas the following day. If the weather is bad, we'll go down to Base Camp and spend a few days while the Col is being stocked.

April 27, Camp 2—This morning came up bright and clear for the first time in a week and a half. Our spirits soared as our thoughts turned to starting the summit assaults at last. Camp 2 has come alive with climbers preparing to move up, up, up. The first assault group of four, with 13 Sherpas, left several hours ago; we'll follow tomorrow, and on the 29th Dingman and Prather will move out with 4 Sherpas to serve as our support party. They'll attempt climbing Lhotse on May 3 if the weather is good. The timetable calls for Whittaker's team to sleep at Camp 3 tonight, Camp 4 tomorrow night, Camp 5 the next night, Camp 6 on the 30th, and then, if the weather is right, they'll shoot for the summit May Day morning. Bishop, Pownall, Girmi, and I will be in the support party at Camp 5, moving up to Camp 6 on May 1 when the first assault team returns. We'll stay at Camp 6 overnight and make our own summit attempt, May 2, while the first team returns to the Col to spend a day on oxygen. Eight of the 13 Sherpas who left here today are scheduled to carry all the way to Camp 6; they'll pack 2 tents, 4 sleeping bags, 22 oxygen bottles, food, and fuel. . . . It's now snowing again. I hope it is only temporary and not another weather front. We will still move to Camp 3 in bad weather as the first group can go to Camp 4. From there to the Col good weather is needed because it really gets windy up there.

April 28, Camp 3—We moved up from Camp 2 at 2 P.M. today and it is a relief to finally be on the move. Just before we left, Ang Pema, whose face was badly lacerated in the accident which killed Jake, came up from Base Camp to Camp 2. His face looked very good, and he said he wants to go to the Col. What a tough little cooky. The weather looked ominous for a while today, but the stars are out now and we are quite optimistic. . . . From here to the summit our fortunes are strictly in the hands of God. The weather is going to play a big role. The 1962 expedition from India was turned around by the wind when it was only 500 feet from the top—and the same can happen to us. Everest up high has a long history of fearful winds, and all we can do is go up there and pray that they won't treat us too unfairly. Now that we are getting closer to our objective the mountain more and more becomes a living, throbbing thing.

April 29, Camp 4—We moved out of Camp 3 at 10 A.M. today and got here at 2:30 P.M. The weather threatened to be bad, and it snowed for about an hour, but by the time we arrived here it was clear. We shot lots of film. I took 100 feet of movie film of the four Sherpas coming off the Col. They reported everyone up there in good shape. Our own four Sherpas did a great job today, and two of them want to accompany us to Camp 6, but they don't have to go, and I don't think there's enough oxygen. The weather is beginning to close in on us again. It is starting to snow and really blowing up a storm, but we are cozy and warm in our sleeping bags and are extremely excited about the prospect of going all the way to the summit.

As Jerstad settled down for the night, he fought back any impulse toward overoptimism, for the world through which they had moved in recent weeks was not merely a world of rock and mist and sunlight and blinding snow, but also a world of psychological warfare, of the unexpected . . . of self-control in the light of constant happenings to mar their progress. Still, what met them at 3 o'clock the following afternoon at Camp 5 was a shattering experience:

We arrived at the South Col today in a fierce wind-storm. What we found was not pleasant. There were only 7 full oxygen bottles and 20 empties, and 10 others had very little oxygen left in them. What a terrible mess! Consequently we must make the most out of what remains. We'll have to change sleeping bottles hourly and cut ourselves down to a mere half liter. We can just about scrape up enough oxygen to get us and the needed reserve oxygen up to Camp 6. This spells doom for any chances of Whittaker's and my climbing Lhotse after we are done on Everest, I'm sure. It is now 7:50 P.M. It has taken us nearly five hours to check over all oxygen bottles, clean up the mess that was left here, and finally get settled. We are just beginning to relax. I wonder what bad luck will befall us next.

The most elaborate plan of conquest ever made for Mount Everest suddenly seemed desperately inadequate to Lute Jerstad. It was only a matter of hours now before they would learn whether they had resources powerful enough to meet the world's mightiest mountain's severest challenge. And history was on its side.

9

Stars and Stripes on Everest

On that night of April 30 the temperature dropped to 5 below zero, and the four climbers at the South Col watched each other's faces for the telltale dead-white patches of frostbite. All their resistance to cold seemed to have vanished. They shivered, and their fingers beat uncontrollable tattoos against everything they touched. It was discouraging to be so much at the mercy of something from which there was no lasting escape.

Lute listened uneasily to the roaring wind

building up outside their tent. He had hoped for a break in the weather, but a stiff gale was whipping up the gorge, lashing snow into weird formations. His fingers were clumsy and writing was a chore, but he felt a need for self-expression:

Man is but a puny animal up here on the Col, all but lost in the immensity of space. Gusts of wind are reaching more than 80 miles an hour. The temperature is below zero and dropping. I hope God is looking benignly down upon lonely climbers this night. We need all the extra help we can get to come out of this alive. We are far out of our league up here.

Barry Bishop stirred, crawled out of his sleeping bag, where he had been trying to keep warm, and stared for a moment out into the churning blackness. He voiced their private fears. "The wind is increasing!"

There is not much for men to do, sitting in a tent at 26,200 feet in a blizzard. Everything that could be done for them had already been done. They made their routine check of supplies. Their oxygen was running low; not enough really. But they would have to make it do.

Lute was unable to sleep. He lay awake in his bag thinking about the chain of events leading up to this uncertain night on Everest. It seemed so long ago now since Norman had called him to Santa Monica to tell him he was coming to Everest with the Americans. So much had happened in the last

105

seven months. So many setbacks—the death of one American, smallpox, accidents, porterage problems, and the relentless walking-climbing, walking-climbing. But hard as the preliminaries had been, they had been able to muster up strength and nerve enough from some deep-down reserve to do what had to be done. Lute transferred his thoughts to his diary again:

My fingers are stiff as clothespins. I can hardly push the pen. The wind continues to howl. It sounds hideous. It sounds like the moaning of a dying man. Inside, the hiss of the stove and oxygen tubes is lost in the roar of the gale. The storm is really punishing us now. Several times it has all but lifted our tent off the ground. Man does not conquer such a mountain as Everest, but is permitted by God to trespass only for a brief time. Not only do the physical elements defeat him, but he defeats himself as well. We might very well lose the summit tomorrow because of a combination of these forces. . . . Why will men subject themselves to such human misery? I cannot explain it. There's a strange almost hypnotic lure about this icy rim of the world, and now that I am up here I feel as though I know something about the mysteries of myself. It gives me an insight I've never felt before. It makes me feel very close to eternity. . . . Our summit strategy for tomorrow is this: Whittaker and Gombu will go first, followed at an hour's interval by Norman and Ang Dawa, who will try to capture as much of the first pair's climb as possible on motion-picture film. We will then move up to Camp 6 and wait, launching our own summit assault just as soon as the first team returns. Of course, a lot can happen between now and tomorrow night.

Lute tried to sleep once more, but sleep wouldn't come. The roaring wind kept him awake. He considered the superstitions that the Sherpas preserved about this mountain. Down the ages they had believed that strange, foreboding spirits guarded the summit against intruders. Lute's mind conjured up a picture of the Americans returning home without putting a single climber on top. Like an aching muscle strained the day before, he carried over into the tent's pitch darkness the painful knot of Western impatience while he waited for dawn. He envied the Sherpas, who did everything so slowly and carelessly and with such infuriating cheerfulness. He inventoried his own frailties. He rarely allowed himself to think about anything else except that great white dome rising 29,028 feet in the air. That was his reason for being there: to scale Everest. The very existence of the mountain had mandated his presence there in that tent. All the way from Katmandu he had been spurred by the lash from an inner voice: "Keep going . . . don't falter . . . up, up, up." There had been little time for any real rest. Pleasures had been few. His sole purpose had been to hurry through each day as if it were his last; as if the world, rich in everything, held out only one prize to him. Was the prize going to be his?

May Day—The wind picked up ferociously at midnight and blew the rest of the night. Some gusts hit
90 miles per hour. Our tent floor raised off the ice
twice, and my feet are quite cold. It will be a miracle
if the Camp 6 gang survives at all. We haven't been
able to make radio contact with Base Camp since
leaving Camp 3. We can receive messages but can't
transmit. It is now 9:30 A.M. and we're waiting for
radio contact from Camp 6—if only they will try
and contact us. I am sure they can't start out for the
summit in this weather, but if by some miracle they
do make it, then we will *try* getting up to Camp 6
and shoot for the summit tomorrow. There's a low-
pressure area sweeping in from Afghanistan today;
that's probably what we are in right now. . . . Because
of our acute shortage of oxygen, only two may be
able to go on. If that happens Pownall has graciously
volunteered to sacrifice his chance at the summit and
let Bishop go instead. We offered to flip a coin to
decide which two of us would go, but Dick said no,
he would stay behind with Girmi and carry for us to
Camp 6. It is an immense personal sacrifice, which
must tear at the very fiber of a man, for Pownall has
worked hard to come this far. What a guy! I hope
Barry and I can go all the way. Time is running out
fast. We might never get this close again. The monsoon may soon hit, and when it does it will wash us
off the mountain. The weather and our decreasing
oxygen supply are the determining factors now.

Lute pulled the hood of his down jacket around
his ears, stepped out into the cold morning air and
scanned the upper Southeast Ridge. Camp 6, dark
and silent, indicated no signs of human life. Lifting

his eyes, Lute gazed at the sky, still cloudy but clearing. The storm and gusty wind was still a serious factor, however. To himself, he questioned the advisability of going through with the morning's scheduled summit assault.

Up at Camp 6, Jim Whittaker had already made his decision. The verdict was GO. He was a bold, imaginative gambler. Early that morning he had stood outside his tent and studied the route he and Gombu would take. The path was deceiving he knew. And a map of Everest wasn't going to be any more enlightening; perhaps that was because the slopes and crevasses, as shown on a map, had been created on a scale so immense that the imagination could not at once grasp them. There, only 1,578 feet from the top, there were no objects of familiar dimensions such as houses and roads and telephone poles by which to measure the background. Now that he was up close, however, Whittaker could clearly tell that the worst of the journey was immediately ahead. Aerial photographic maps could indeed be misleading!

Norman Dyhrenfurth was pleased when Whittaker announced he had decided to take Gombu and try for the top. Norman later wrote: "As for myself, I had no illusion about getting to the summit." In six days he would be celebrating his 45th birthday. He also had a responsibility to the expedition as leader. Those factors, combined with his

50-pound load of oxygen and camera equipment, ruled out any ambition to climb to the top of Everest. Ang Dawa and Norman would go as high as they could to be in a favorable position to photograph Whittaker and Gombu standing on the Main Summit.

Jim looked at his watch.

"Six o'clock."

"Good luck, Jim."

"Thanks. We'll try it."

Whittaker's confidence was based on several factors. He knew that they had carefully nursed their reserve strength on the lower part of the mountain; they had acclimatized gradually, working hard enough to keep their muscles in condition without wearing them out before the final assault. He was also aware of the fact that, at 34, he was at the very height of his own physical powers. Six feet five inches, rangy, habitually relaxed both in body and temperament, Whittaker possessed a dogged endurance that at times seemed to approach the superhuman. He also knew that the 27-year-old, barrelchested Gombu had strength and the desire to go on in the face of adversity. Everest was his dream, too. If the little Sherpa could not raise himself to the ultimate pinnacle by legs and lungs alone, then he would do it by the power of his indomitable spirit.

At 6:15 A.M., all was ready. Imperceptibly the sky began to lighten in the east. The slopes and ridges took substance where an hour ago they had been only a blacker part of the boiling night. Gombu shifted his pack nervously, eager to be moving. Jim said good-bye to Norman and Ang Dawa and then, head down, plowed off through the wind and snow. Under the weight of every step the snow crunched and groaned and flying ice roared about them like artillery. Following its normal pattern, the howling wind worsened the higher they crept. But come what might, they had committed themselves now. It was too late to turn back. . . .

More than a thousand feet below Camp 6, Jerstad, Bishop, Pownall, and Girmi Dorje waited a long day out. At 1:45 P.M., Lute parked himself outside his tent and scanned the upper ridges. His private thoughts at that moment are revealed in his diary:

Until about half an hour ago, the wind blew furiously; 50–60 mph gale force and gusts up to 80. The temperature at 8 A.M. was 18 degrees below zero! It is —4 now and snowing again. Without radio contact we were forced to stay here today. We don't know what's going on up at Camp 6. At noon we saw two figures coming down at about 28,000 feet. They were moving very slowly. We couldn't tell through the mist who they were. We're going out of our minds wondering what is happening up there. Moreover, we are almost out of oxygen and must move tomorrow. We have little oxygen and sleep on only half-liters at night to conserve it. It's bitter cold, and I'm freezing. . . . We wish we knew what's going on upstairs. The tension is maddening. If the figures we saw earlier were Jim and Gombu, they surely are powerful if they got to the summit, because climbing conditions are unbelievably bad. The altitude is beginning to affect our minds, I think. In a note we sent down with Sherpas two days ago, we neglected to mention that our radio transmission had gone haywire. Another example of this lapse of memory is that I had my oxygen mask, camera, and string from my down mittens all fouled up last night, and Barry had to help me untangle the mess. I simply couldn't figure it out for myself.

Lute's vision, unfortunately, had deceived him earlier in the day. For all the good a man's eyes did him in the thick mist, he might as well have kept them closed. Lute had been correct about seeing two men up at 28,000 feet, but they were Norman and Ang Dawa. All that morning they had bucked violent wind and driven snow along the ever-rising slope, plodding in the footsteps of Whittaker and Gombu. They had progressed only 750 feet by noon, and the main phase of the slope was yet to be tackled. Up and up and up, for nearly five hours they had labored, single file; now on a sharp ridge, now traversing a broad hogback of ice and snow, with the crest of the jagged peak still looming above. At 28,200 feet, Norman stopped. He was panting. His face was turning blue. Their oxygen was almost gone. Behind Norman came Ang Dawa's voice.

"Up Sahib."

Norman shook his head.

"No, we're finished."

Ang Dawa pointed to the South Summit, only 550 feet away. That had been their goal. It offered a spectacular position from which to shoot movies of the Main Summit. But the frightful weather made photography impossible. There was no purpose in going on. The tone of Norman's voice carried authority: "We're going back down."

For Norman Dyhrenfurth, it was the end of a cherished dream. Never again would he come so near to the highest pinnacle on earth. He gained small solace in the knowledge that no man his age had ever climbed that high. Reluctantly, Norman and Ang Dawa turned around and started down.

Meanwhile, above them, the drama continued. . . .

Whittaker and Gombu sat on the South Summit, pausing to rest. They surveyed the route to the top. The raging wind still howled across the upper reaches of Everest. Though Jim could make out the upper crest, it was difficult for him to estimate the distance. His guess was 300 feet, give or take a few. The route was steeper than he had imagined, and negotiating the final North Ridge would be no cinch. But he was positive that they had finished the toughest part of the climb. Below them, the traveling had been painfully slow and miserable. Knee-deep snowdrifts had added to the burden and uncounted hundreds of steps had had to be chopped in the glazed trail all the way up the unrelieved steepness of the ridge. The snow was loose and unstable in places and the footing was dangerous. One false step would have plunged them thousands of feet into the abyss below. All the way up from Camp 6 they had traded leads, cutting steps, then stopping, resting momentarily, and belaying the rope. Again and again they had repeated this one-at-a-time maneuver until they stood together 278 feet from the summit.

Slowly, they got up, refastened their straps, and moved on. At 28,500 feet, just below the South Summit, they had unloaded a bottle of oxygen apiece to lighten their packs, but they had each held onto a second bottle. Now they adjusted their regulators on these second bottles so that they would have full bottles to travel the rest of the way on. The wind was strong and punishing as they moved upward. Drifts of snow piled up in front of them as they picked their way between rock and the acute cornices dropping off to the east. A very delicate margin had to be maintained because if they edged too far out on the cornice it would avalanche; on the other hand, their crampons slipped on rock. Carefully they inched their way up, belaying one another at frequent intervals, while limiting themselves to an oxygen flow of 3 liters.

The last several hundred feet seemed endless to the exhausted climbers. They dropped 30 feet to a saddle between the ridge and North Summit, and this was a place where inches of altitude had great stature. With extreme self-control they labored toward the base of the North Summit, belaying one another, moving one at a time. Once they were safely at the base, Whittaker stopped and stared briefly at those final feet of ice, snow, and rock. He motioned to Gombu to follow him. Together they worked their way toward the North Summit. They were only 15 minutes and a few feet from their goal now. They toiled on for endless inches; important inches and each a torment. Suddenly, where alternately there had been rock and snow, there was only snow. Only a dome. Only a hump suspended in sky. Whittaker turned to Gombu and signaled for him to stop.

"You go first, Gombu."

Gombu shook his head vigorously. The Sherpa objected to the honor of being the first to step onto the summit.

"No! You—you go first."

The hump of snow was wide enough for two men. Whittaker settled the question by grabbing hold of Gombu's elbow and steering him those last few feet. Beyond, everything else fell away. Jim slapped Gombu on the back. They hugged each other. Jim then dug his ice ax into the snow and slung his pack over it. Tears streamed down his haggard face. *He was the first American in history to stand at the top of Everest.* But as he was to confess later, he felt neither expansive nor sublime in that moment of victory. He felt merely like a frail human being.

There, at 1 P.M. on May 1, 1963, a big man from

115

the West and a small man from the East stood together in space—two tiny dots as alone as two men could possibly be. Three years of careful planning, tons of equipment, 908 porters, 37 specialized Sherpas, 19 American climbers, and $400,000 had combined to put them there.

With the wind blowing mightily and the temperature sagging to −30 degrees, Jim and Gombu fought against time before starting down. Jim pulled from his pack a 4-foot aluminum stake with an American flag attached to it and planted it in the snow. That gesture made their victory official. Old Glory ripped and tore wildly in the wind, but it held. Jim pulled out his still camera and snapped pictures of the flag. Then he and Gombu took turns photographing each other holding other smaller flags: of the United States, of Nepal, of the National Geographic Society, of the Himalayan Institute of Mountaineering in Darjeeling, India, where Gombu was a staff instructor; and of Gombu holding a *kata*, the traditional "friendship scarf" of the Buddhist faith (similar to one later presented as a gift from the expedition to President John F. Kennedy). Whittaker and Gombu took pictures of the world on all sides of the summit: of the summits of Makalu, Lhotse, Nuptse, and all the other great giants, thousands of feet below them as if in another world, and of the Tibetan plateau flattened interminably to the north. They had literally climbed out of the storm below them, and the breathtaking view afforded

116

them on top of Everest was one they will carry for the rest of their lives.

What a moment to run out of oxygen. But that's what happened. They had miscalculated, estimating that one bottle apiece would take them round-trip from 28,500 feet to the summit and return. They had only those few minutes on the summit. It was time to leave.

They dumped their empty tanks and started down. Minus oxygen, the pace was more arduous now. They had gone only a short distance when the first of several major crises arose. On their way up to the summit they had followed the ridge line where rock (now on their right) met snow (now on their left), but with Gombu taking the lead on the way back down, he veered farther over on the snow than necessary, causing a whole section of the cornice between them to dissolve and fall away—all the way into Tibet over 10,000 feet beneath them!

They slogged on for two hours, oxygenless and beaten. The subzero temperature froze the water in their canteens, and now dehydration was an unwanted traveling companion. But they could not quit. They crawled on; belaying each other; moving one at a time; moving half a rope length; stopping to gain breath; gasping for air; moving once more, groping for position to belay.

At Camp 5, Lute looked at his wristwatch. Five P.M. They had stayed close to camp all day hoping

117

for some word from the men at Camp 6. His anxiety of that hour can be found in his diary. At 5:15 P.M., he wrote:

We have just spotted two figures crawling down below the South Summit. They must be Jim and Gombu. They are moving very slowly, stopping often. They appear beat; must be out of oxygen. We still have no idea whether or not they got to the summit, because our radio is on the blink. We assume they made it, however.

In the majority of books written about Everest there are references to "attacks" on Everest and "assaults" on Everest, but none of those terms aptly describes the nightmare experienced by Whittaker and Gombu. They were like sleepwalkers fumbling aimlessly in another world. Each step of their return was won only at the price of parched throats and gasping, burning lungs.

At last, the two climbers, drained of all human endurance, staggered into Camp 6. The time was 5:50 P.M. They had been gone exactly 12 hours and 35 minutes. There was strength enough in them only to give a feeble victory signal to Norman and Ang Dawa—and then they collapsed in their sacks to sleep the night out. In the ominous world above them, only one thing moved that night: the American flag on the summit of Everest.

Jerstad was up bright and early on the morning of May 2, pacing back and forth nervously in front

118

Barry C. Bishop, © National Geographic Society

After viewing this scene, Jerstad wrote in his diary: "There it stands. Everest. Its pyramid thrusts savagely into the blue sky like a great white monster. Its gigantic plume of snow at the summit, buffeted by fierce winds, presents an incredible sight. . . ."

Luther G. Jerstad, AMEE

No roads lead to the top of Everest. The journey to the summit poses one obstacle after another. One misstep often means sudden disaster. Here a Sherpa moves past a seemingly bottomless pit.

Up, up, up into the lonely world of ice and snow on Everest.

Barry Prather rests at Base Camp, basking in the sunshine and reading a book appropriately entitled *Endurance*.

Bishop gets ready to fasten on his crampons and start up to Camp 3 (22,900 feet) on Everest's South Col route.

Lute Jerstad and Dick Pownall appear as mere specks heading from Camp 2 to Camp 3.

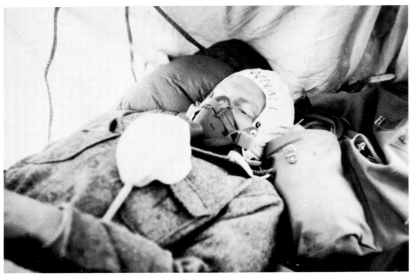

Above 22,900 feet, it was necessary for the climbers to learn to sleep in the thin air with oxygen masks on.

Between Camp 4 and Camp 5 on the South Col route the climbers were forced to move slowly and take six gulps of air between steps. Here Dick Pownall surveys the route upward.

Luther G. Jerstad, AMEE

Gazing into the West Cwm from Camp 4 (24,900 feet), Jerstad and Bishop were able to look down on 23,442-foot Pumori, the pyramid above the clouds. On the right, Everest's icy west shoulder plunges into the valley.

Luther G. Jerstad, AMEE

Sherpas, having delivered oxygen to Camp 4, descend into the Cwm, leaving Jerstad and Bishop alone.

of his tent. He still hadn't been able to get a rise out of the men up at Camp 6. At 9 A.M., he wrote in his diary:

I've tried yelling, screaming, mental telepathy, and running around in the snow in an effort to attract attention at Camp 6 and get them to radio us. Nothing has worked. We still don't know what's going on up there. We intend to strike out for Camp 6 in about an hour. I don't know if we will make it. Right now I'm trying to chew a breakfast of Grape-Nuts and coconut. I can hardly get it down. I have no appetite. We spent a distressing night. At 3 A.M., we ran out of our night's allotment of oxygen and had to spend the rest of the night without any. Pownall grew very cold and shaky. You get cold in a hurry when that oxygen goes off; without it I got only about an hour's sleep. Despite going two nights on the South Col with practically no oxygen, we remain in fairly good shape. Pownall is steadily losing his enthusiasm, though; he has been through more than I. If many more setbacks hit us, such as finding a low oxygen supply at Camp 6, we may throw in the towel. We have just about reached the breaking point.

If those moments were bad at Camp 5, they were even more depressing for the men at Camp 6. Whittaker's oxygen supply had been exhausted soon after midnight and he had spent the rest of the night gasping for air. Norman's supply was also gone, and he was suffering from high-altitude sickness. Acute bodily deterioration was overcoming him. He had been up there too long.

119

Jim and Gombu left early to stop the Camp 5 party from advancing to Camp 6. The oxygen was all gone, so there was no longer sanity in any continuation of the climbing schedule.

Lute's diary contains the details of what followed:

It's 2 P.M. on what was supposed to be *the* day and bad luck continues to plague us like a hideous dream. Logistics broke down, there's been sickness, and the weather fouled. Just as we started up to Camp 6 today we saw two of the first bunch coming down. We pushed on anyway, because we still had four full reserve bottles of oxygen left, enough to get us to the summit and back. In spite of all the reversals, we were confident of success. We had traveled about 200 feet when we met Whittaker and Gombu. The physical nightmare they had been through was written on their faces. Jim resembled an old man, 30 years older. His face was heavily lined, his eyes were bloodshot, and his skin was blue. I've never seen a man age so much in so few hours in all my life. Gombu didn't look much better. We immediately revived them with our oxygen. Finally, Jim was able to talk. Yes, they had climbed Everest. The weather was frightful. They had left at 6:15 A.M. and reached the top at 1 P.M. They ran out of oxygen while on top and only by sheer superhuman effort were they able to get back down alive. It was a 12-hour day, part of which was spent between 29,028 feet and 28,400 feet without oxygen! It has to be put down as one of the great Himalayan efforts. After helping Jim and Gombu back to our tent and settling them on oxygen, Barry and I decided to try a two-man assault on the summit. But first we would wait for Norman and Ang Dawa to come down. When they still hadn't appeared after two hours, we grew fidgety. Both Jim and Gombu, their feet hurting from possible frostbite, were anxious to start down, but they refused to go until they were sure Norman was safe. I was inside the tent talking to Jim and Gombu when Bishop spotted them. We quickly pulled on our boots and rushed off to meet them. Norman had been 10 hours without oxygen and was delirious. He kept calling me Dave. The minute I got to him he collapsed. I shouted down to Pownall to hurry and bring oxygen. Norman was subsequently revived there in the snow, relieved of his pack, and helped back to the tent, where we put him on a full flow of oxygen. Ang Dawa received the same treatment. And that ended our summit dreams then and there. We had no choice. They needed our oxygen. We are leaving now to take Norman and Ang Dawa down to lower elevation. Barry, Girmi, and I stayed behind while Whittaker, Pownall, and Gombu left earlier for Camp 2.

And so five beaten men with red eyes, scraggly beards, and haggard faces started down. Lute lingered for a final moment, his gaze lifted toward the great white dome—so near and yet so far.

"I stood there," Lute said, "vowing to myself, 'I'll be back . . . I'll be back,' and actually I was wondering if I ever would. We were playing tag with danger."

10

Encore: Four Are Chosen

On May 4, the day after coming back down from Camp 5, Lute sat in his tent at Base Camp writing letters and catching up on his diary. The struggle against the mountain was going into its 75th day, and the men had grown befogged. They were just plain worn out, mentally as well as physically. They had drained their emotions until much of the desire to succeed on Everest left them, and the dreams they dreamed were no longer of summits but of home. What they needed was a change, something to freshen their outlook and restore their perspective.

Lute felt like an old man. The perpetual, choking altitude, the muscle-stiffening cold air, the snatched food sitting heavy on the stomach, the inner drive to go, go, go, hour after hour, and on through the next day, and the next, had taken the stamina out of him. The process had started gradually, a little at a time, and at last had worked into an emotional tapestry of one long, confusing pattern—yesterday is tomorrow, east is north and south is west, and when will it all be over?

Climbing Everest was so romantic—if you were far away from it!

Most expeditions would have folded their tents and gone home. But not the Americans. They were still affluent in manpower and equipment, and since Whittaker and Gombu had reached the summit early in the year, some good climbing weather remained. It was quickly decided to go ahead with the final phase of the campaign. This would consist of two simultaneous assaults: one by Lute and Bishop from the South Col route, and the other by Willi and Tom via the unconquered West Ridge. It would be the grandstand play to end all grandstand plays. Lacking his former enthusiasm, Lute wrote in his diary:

I'm getting sick of this mountain. Whittaker and Gombu are really sick of it. I still feel low after miss-

123

ing our first big chance at the summit. We'll stay here a week before starting back up again. We really need the rest. I now weigh only 132 pounds. I've lost 26. This will be my third trip to the Col—and I hope there's truth in the old saying that the third time is a charm. I don't think I could take another failure. We are going to have to make this last shot good, because the Sherpas are really dragging and can't keep carrying high much longer. As for Norman's condition after his close call on May Day, he is feeling better. I think he will be okay. Prather suffered a bad pulmonary edema attack at Camp 4 on the way down, and if Dingman hadn't been with him, he probably would have been a fatality. . . . We still haven't told Katmandu who the first two men were that got to the summit. The world's newspapers are really after us now to give out the names, but at the start of the expedition we agreed among ourselves that if any of us reached the top our identity would remain a secret until ALL attempts had been completed. In that way ALL the fellows here would share equally in the credit for victory. But how long we can keep the names of Whittaker and Gombu a secret under the growing pressure of world curiosity is open to doubt. I hope they'll be able to add the names of Bishop, Unsoeld, Hornbein, and Jerstad to that list before very long. We're all anxious to go home.

May 5, Base Camp—The weather is good in the mornings, then clouds up and snows in the afternoons. The A.M. would be ideal for a summit attempt. Hornbein and Unsoeld left today for the West Ridge, and Barry and I expect to leave on May

11 in time to coordinate our assault with theirs. We have just enough oxygen, 26 bottles, to get to the summit and back.

May 6, Base Camp—We were awakened at 6 A.M. for tea this morning. What an ungodly hour when one is here to rest! Whittaker, Pownall, and Doody got haircuts from Passang Temba today, and they look good. I need a haircut too but will wait until I come off the summit. This crop of long hair will keep my ears warm up there. I'm taking only enough gear and clothes to last 10 days this trip. . . . Will Siri continues to use us as human guinea pigs, and he's running radioactive iron through some of the guys today.

May 7, Base Camp—Another beautiful day and we're still sitting here at Base Camp. I only hope the weather holds out. Trying to keep the names of the first summit team from the newspapers is causing Jim Ullman [in Katmandu] all sorts of headaches. Both Whittaker and Gombu are anxious to let their wives know of their success, but their secrecy was agreed upon in February, and Jim Ullman is only doing his duty. Bishop and I are determined to go as far as we are physically capable of going.

May 8, Base Camp—In three more days Barry and I will be on our way. At the moment the weather is slightly deteriorating. Maybe it will improve before we begin the actual final assault. There's a low-pressure area moving this way, and it may provide us with the lull we need. Physically, I have been feeling stronger in this thicker air and have gained two and a half pounds. I've been drinking plenty of liquids and don't feel nearly as dehydrated as I get when I'm up higher. Down here I don't have to take sleeping pills to rest.

May 9, Base Camp—Just two more days. The tension is beginning to grow inside of us now. I hope the weather will give us a break. The old spirit is returning, and we really want that summit now. For the last 36 hours it has been snowing, but the atmosphere should clear once we get to higher ground. We'll probably start up in bad weather and pray that good conditions prevail at Camp 6. If nature turns against us, we are through and will toss in the towel. It's a great feeling to realize that this tedious battle against the mountain is almost over—and a relief to know we will soon be able to forget animal-like survival. Man wasn't meant to exist this way. . . . Sixteen Sherpas have returned to Camp 3 West. The weather has been uncomfortably poor, but the fellows are making headway up on the West Ridge. Barry and I will take only four Sherpas with us to the Col, and two of them will carry oxygen for us to Camp 6. I am taking a New Testament my family sent me. I thought of leaving it on the summit if we get that far, but I doubt if I will. It means more to me in my pocket.

May 10, Base Camp—After nine days, and with all sorts of rumors, true and false, in circulation, it became necessary last night for Jim Ullman to give out the names of Whittaker and Gombu to the press. That makes it official now. We are very hopeful of adding four more names to the list. After all, it is only good housekeeping for us to go back up there and make sure that the first assault team's aluminum

Maypole is still standing tall and straight. I'll be wearing my lucky shorts.

May 11, Base Camp—We delayed going to Camp 2 today because of a request from the fellows on the West Ridge. They said to wait until the 12th, then tonight they wanted us to wait two more days. We are growing very impatient and want to be moving. I don't think we can give them support even if we should hit the same summit day. Our chances of meeting on the summit of Everest are about 1 in 500, or less. We are afraid that the longer we wait the bigger the odds against our making it. We have been cheated out of our summit success, and we are afraid it could happen again. I am very willing to help the West Ridgers, but the traverse [crossing the summit from one side to the other] has always frightened me and I don't think we, in our marginal state of oxygen supply, would do much good. In bad weather Tom and Willi would be extremely lucky to find our Camp 6. . . . Jim Lester and Gil Roberts came down to Base Camp tonight. Gil had been at Camp 2 for six weeks, which must certainly be close to a record for staying at over 21,000 feet. We were there one month and a few days. . . . We do not know what awaits us on the mountain, we only hope we can make it and not succumb. Men never know the fury or the sublimity of themselves or their environment until they meet it. The plans of mice and men—who knows how we will come down—changed—normal—strengthened—weakened—we only pray that we come down.

May 12, Camp 1—Bishop and I romped up here today in 1 hour and 50 minutes. I carried only 15

127

pounds, and Barry had no pack at all. It was a breeze. After we got here we helped Maynard Miller with some glaciology, and tomorrow we will help him set a ladder over a crevasse edge. Sherpas Nima Tensing, Girmi Dorje, and Kalden, all good men, are here too. Just before bedtime a huge avalanche roared off the West Ridge and went crashing clear across the Cwm. One of the Sherpas grabbed his ice ax and fled for his life, but we shouted after him, "It's okay—no worry!" and he came back. I guess we all are frightened by them no matter how often we see them. They remind a man of his insignificance up in this untamed world.

May 13, Camp 2—We helped Maynard install a ladder over a crevasse today so he can get samples, then we ate lunch and left for Camp 2. We arrived here in two hours. It was another pleasant, leisurely stroll. We are saving our strength for when we are really going to need it. . . . Emerson and Corbet met us and we talked over the West Ridge versus South Col route problem and ironed out some details.

May 14, Camp 2—Barry and I were all prepared to push off for Camp 3 this morning but were persuaded to wait several more days to coincide with the West Ridge team's ascent. The plan, of course, is for Barry and me to meet Willi and Tom on the summit—history! The date for the final assault is now set for May 21. Over our radio today it sounded as if the West Ridgers lost a day. We don't know for sure. Any delay on their part could be serious now. If we wait much longer, we will get clobbered by the monsoon. We have promised to wait here until the 17th but no longer. Our Sherpas are champing at the bit to get going. They think we are crazy for waiting, because the West Ridge team could hit all sorts of technical problems. . . . Dave Dingman and Pemba Tensing will come up here tomorrow and serve as our support party. Then we can move out at any time. We have only enough oxygen to carry out the assault. Our confidence remains high. I am really carrying a light load this trip: two shirts, down underwear, parka, pants, six pairs of socks, sleeping bag, and ensolite pad. That's all. . . . Two Sherpas came down from the West Ridge a while ago quite sick. They reported that 12 loads were carried to Camp 4 West and that Willi and Al Auten will stay there tonight. They will try to establish Camp 5 West (27,250 feet) tomorrow or the next day. They are apparently right on schedule. We'll talk to them via radio tonight at 6 P.M.

May 15, Camp 2—We've been taking it easy today. Corbet and Emerson started up for the West Ridge, but Dick suddenly grew sick and Corbet went on alone. Emerson has been exposed to high altitude too long, and his body won't take much more. Dingman and Maynard Miller are supposed to join us today, but it is now 3:15 P.M. and there's still no sign of them. We need them. We ran out of kerosene last night and had a cold breakfast. Lunch was even colder—none! The weather is beautiful right now. Inside the tents now the temperature is warm as toast, and I curled up a while ago and slept for an hour or so. The premonsoon lull is definitely here, and we're praying for at least a week of good weather. Our three Sherpas carried eight oxygen bottles to Camp 3 today and brought down all the tents except two four-man tents. We intend to bring the sleeping bags and tents down from Camp 4 upon our re-

129

turn from the summit. We will abandon the three four-man tents on the Col, thus adding to the world's highest junkyard. They have stood up under tremendous pounding from the wind; the fabric has been separated in places but not ripped. . . . Our Sherpas still think we are foolish not to be moving up in such ideal weather. I agree with them, but we promised to wait here until the 17th. I think I will cry if both teams hit bad weather, because we would have been on our way to 25,000 feet by now if we hadn't waited. All we can do in the meantime is sit tight, hope—and pray. We must not forget that the West Ridgers are fighting a tougher battle than we are, and we would be selfish, indeed, to refuse to wait for them.

May 16, Camp 2—Dick Emerson, despite his physical condition, went back up toward Camp 3 West alone this morning and after four hours has gone only a third of the way. He is making very slow progress, and darkness will soon fall. He had better turn around and come back down. . . . Unsoeld and Hornbein were supposed to scout a route to find a site for Camp 5 West today. That's over 27,000 feet. They are facing fierce winds up there now, and we don't know if they got very far. A weather front with powerful gusts is starting to slash us now, and it doesn't look promising.

Turbulence and chaos were written in the western sky that night, and the members of the South Col party scurried to lash down every loose article in sight. Then they waited for the storm to hit. It hit, all right, a genuine rouser this time, detonating over Everest like an atom bomb, with purposeful streaks of lightning, and torrents of swirling ice hissing across the tent tops. Then snow covered Camp 2, forcing the men to dig in to keep from being buried.

Over on the West Ridge the situation was even more serious. . . .

For some six hours the "high" storm fell with all its fury on Camp 4 West. It wasn't until midnight that the four Americans and four Sherpas there realized to their horror that the storm was blowing two tents downhill—with Barry Corbet and Al Auten and the Sherpas still in their sacks! Food boxes, equipment, and oxygen bottles bounced around like Ping-Pong balls as the sliding tents gained momentum. The wind was blowing them toward Everest's North Face, a plunge of 6,000 feet, and beyond that plunge, miles of glacier sloping off into Tibet. Fortunately the tents lodged themselves in a shallow hollow about 100 feet below Camp 4 West.

For minutes all was a wild, noisy scene of ripped nylon, jutting poles, strewn gear, and startled, struggling men, yet Unsoeld and Hornbein were unaware of developments. They were still pinned down in another tent up at the original campsite. They had heard nothing outside but the howl of the deafening storm. Some time elapsed before Al Auten was able to crawl back up the ridge to tell Tom and Willi what had been happening. The three of them then fought their way down to the tent wreckage. The scene was a shambles.

Spirits were low as the men bound what remained of the ravaged tents with lengths of rope and anchored them as best they could, then settled back to wait out the rest of the storm. It roared and fumed undiminished the rest of the night. At 9 A.M. the next morning, it still hadn't abated. In the lone tent still standing at 4 West, Hornbein, Corbet, and Unsoeld cranked up their walkie-talkie and radioed Base Camp. Willi was in the middle of giving his storm report when he felt a sharp jerk. The tent was moving!

"Tom—Barry—get out! We're going down!"

Within minutes all remnants of what had been Camp 4 West were reduced to ruin. An hour later eight sad-faced men, their emotions and bodies spent, slogged back down to 3 West in silence. On the way down, Willi kept telling himself: "We've had it. There's no chance of making it up the West Ridge now. It's all over." He went to bed that night feeling blackly discouraged.

Tom Hornbein did not share Willi's defeatism. He stayed awake the rest of the night thinking, and the following morning he was armed to the teeth with a host of solutions.

"You know," he said, "what we're going to have to do is skip a camp."

He had the details all figured out: how many porters they would require, how much oxygen was left, and what would have to be left behind. The other men agreed that his plan had merit. They would take as many porters as they could get (they wanted five but would settle for three) and move back up the mountain as soon as they could get the Sherpas in position. They would also need an extra box of food and another Gerry tent to replace the one that had been blown down in the storm.

They needed only a minimum of extra equipment. There was plenty of oxygen in place at 4 West, and tentage problems could be solved by moving up two of Camp 3 West's three tents. The crux of the plan was to carry what they could from Camp 4 West all the way up to what was originally going to be 6 West, skip the intermediate camp and go 2,000 feet instead of 1,000. It would require a rugged carry but it was their only chance.

It was worth a try, and for the next two days the men recuperated from the storm. Willi later confessed he was more exhausted during those several days than at any other period on Everest. He had doubts about his ability to go on. He just wanted to sleep and read. He had no energy and no ambition. Willi was being very honest with himself, because Dick Emerson had raised the question of which two men would be on the summit team.

Dick said, "Let's decide right now who's going."

"To my mind," Barry Corbet spoke up, "there's no question about it. In terms of work put in on the route, stamina, and general background, it has to be Willi and Tom."

"I agree," Emerson said.

Willi had doubts about his stamina. He had

been working steadily day after day on the West Ridge route, breaking trail and leading the reconnaissance with Hornbein, and now he was bushed. A provisional choice was made subsequently: if Willi was able to go, he would join Hornbein; if not, Barry Corbet would replace him. That settled it.

After resting for two days Willi perked up, and on May 20 he felt he was strong enough to go with Tom. They left fairly late that day because it was a moderately easy carry from 3 West to 4 West. The snow was in excellent condition after the beating it had absorbed from the storm, and they had no problem chopping out steps. They moved up quickly to the crest of the ridge, but once there, Willi discovered he had left his ultraviolet filter on another camera lens back at 3 West. It was necessary for high-altitude photography, so after a great deal of soul-searching he dropped his pack and hurried back down for it, feeling very disgusted with himself. He picked up that insignificant little piece of glass, tucked it in his pocket, and hoisted an extra bottle of oxygen onto his back. He hooked the bottle to his mask, gave himself a 4-liter flow of air, and went charging up the hill to Tom. From the crest to 3 West and back up again, with time out for lunch, the trip took an hour and seven minutes.

While Willi went back for his camera filter, Tom sat on the crest of the ridge and waited. He valued that hour as much as any other single hour spent on Everest. It gave him the solitude his soul craved, and was heightened by a magnificent view. He had been alone so seldom since leaving the United States. Barry Corbet and Dick Emerson and the Sherpas had moved off, and he was totally alone with his thoughts. This opportunity was of inestimable value to Tom, and by the time Willi returned he was in great spirits. They really traveled after that, moving up with light packs and plenty of oxygen.

They spent the night at 4 West, and set out the next morning for 5 West, a fantastic carry over extremely difficult terrain and twice the ordinary one-day distance. Corbet and Auten were the first to leave, at 6:50 A.M. The Sherpas were then hooked up to their oxygen and loaded with food, sleeping bags, and air mattresses. One Sherpa, Ila Tsering, demurred slightly when he picked up the heavy food box. He already had on a 50-pound pack, and in feeling the weight of the box, he groaned, "Oh, very heavy load, Sahib. No can carry this high." And he put it back down. He thought for a moment, then said, "Oh, well, last carry. I take," and he picked it up again. Hornbein and Unsoeld and Emerson waited at Camp 4 West to give the others a head start, and while they were killing time Dick spoke up: "Say, what's the purpose of my being up here?" He was obviously perturbed somewhat at not being given any special job to do. Willi explained to him that three of the Sherpas were very inexperienced, and if any of them collapsed Dick would be needed to take over the load. That seemed to satisfy Dick, and the three of them hooked up their oxygen and started off. The climbers made good time. Corbet, in the lead, and Auten, following, were by now cutting steps in the couloir's steep snow. The Sherpas were not far behind.

After two hours of steady climbing, Tom, Willi, and Dick reached the base of a big snow-filled gully leading straight up. Willi had named it "Hornbein's Couloir," and the elevation was 26,200 feet. That was their route, and it marked the end of the line for Emerson. He had been pushing himself unmercifully, going on will power and desire alone, and now he could not take another step.

He told Willi and Tom, "I'll wait here. I don't want to hold you up. Corbet and Auten and the Sherpas can pick me up on their way back down. I'll be okay."

Willi and Tom went on. Some hours later their ascent stopped. At 27,240 feet they found the first possible site to pitch their tent, a platform of snow just big enough to hold a single two-man tent. The carry was completed. The last thing Willi and Tom remembered was Al Auten starting back down, turning briefly to wave one last good-by, and saying, "Good luck." And then they were alone. . . .

For a full day and night hurricane winds had hammered away at the South Col, and Lute and Barry and the others had sought cover under nylon until the storm passed on. Of the storm, Lute's diary says:

May 17, Camp 2—Barry, Dingman, Jimmy Roberts, and I were in the mess tent when the weather broke loose. The tent blew down, and we were all entangled in pots, pans, food tins, and nylon. It really shakes you up when you suddenly realize that all that stands between you and 80-mile-per-hour winds and flying ice is one little piece of cloth. No one panicked, however. Maynard Miller fought his way through the storm with batteries for our radio. What an unselfish person; he was willing to risk life and limb for us. Seeing Camp 2 upon his arrival, he thought we had been hit by a bomb. Our tents were either half-standing or completely flattened. The wind stopped at about 5 P.M. today. . . . Dick Emerson was on his way to Camp 3 West and was forced to bivouac in a crevasse at 22,600 feet on the West Ridge. After the wind died down, he went on again. We had given him up for dead when Camp 3 West radioed us that Dick hadn't yet shown up at 8:15 A.M.

May 18, Camp 3—We hiked to Camp 3 in three hours today. Halfway here I began feeling ill. I hope it's only because I haven't eaten hot food for several days and not that I *have just had it*. When we arrived it became apparent that an avalanche had hit this place, probably yesterday. One of our four-man draw-tite tents took a direct hit by a chunk of flying ice, mangling the frame, but the nylon held. We repitched it closer to the ice wall. The food and oxygen were buried but not swept away. We had to

137

dig with our hands until the Sherpas arrived with a shovel. I am very tired tonight. I hope I don't slow Barry up. I have never felt like this on a mountain before. Barry has been kind and patient with me and has offered to break trail all day tomorrow. Maybe all I need is a good night's sleep. To keep up my morale while slogging up here, I tried reciting poetry. I have memorized poems at 23,000 feet just to see if it is possible. It seems to be.

May 19, Camp 4—We left Camp 3 at 10:45 A.M. and got here at 4:15 P.M. The snow was up to Barry's neck at the first fixed rope, forcing us to shovel out a path. I felt much better today, and we alternated back and forth on the lead until Barry began suffering cramps in his stomach, similar to those I had yesterday. We found Camp 4 in about the same mess Camp 3 had been in after the storm. One of the tents was filled with snowdrift, sleeping bags were damp, and we consumed a lot of precious time and energy digging out. I am writing this by a candle lantern and can hardly see. It is below zero tonight and quite miserable outside. We plan to go on to the South Col in the morning.

May 20, Midway to Camp 5—We are resting here halfway between Camps 4 and 5. So far it has been a terrible struggle. Some of the fixed ropes are buried under so much snow we have had to burn up priceless energy wrenching them free—energy we had been saving for later. We are packing heavy loads, and the Sherpas are just plain iron men. They are carrying 60 to 70 pounds without the aid of oxygen. Barry and I are toting about 55 pounds apiece but are on oxygen. We are eating up our minds worrying about the state of the tents on the Col. Are they still standing after that vicious storm? We have no idea what we will find. We have been discussing the possibility of shooting all the way from Camp 4 to Camp 6 in one day if it develops that Camp 5 has been wiped out.

The pace up to Camp 5 was unbelievable. The climbers were forced to cling and draw themselves up a foot at a time. It was one breath at a time now, one breath on top of the next, but each breath was an inch closer to the goal. They sometimes slipped, and they sometimes tumbled back, kicking and trying desperately to catch hold again, spurring into the snow to break themselves to a stop. Then they started uphill once more. The strain and physical punishment had the men worn down like old knife blades. Legs stiff and backs stiff, Lute and Barry stopped an hour later to rest and compare notes. They still hadn't spotted Camp 5. Lute said, "We're coming in lower this time than we did before."

Barry said he knew approximately where Camp 5 should have been, but the last time he had been up there the icy glacier above the Col was covered by snow and now it was bare. This confused him. "Let's go find those tents," he said, and disappeared suddenly over a little ridge. When he reappeared he was grinning and wildly flailing his arms around. Lute wondered if he had gone crazy. But Barry was perfectly sane. He had spotted the tents. The South Col assault was very much in business again.

That night Lute wrote in his diary:

Several hours ago Kalden [a Sherpa] began complaining of pains. He was breathing hard. Down at Camp 4 he had had a scab on his leg and I cleaned it for him, then gave him a shot of penicillin and radioed Base Camp for additional instructions. They said we had done the right thing. So tonight we called down again and were advised to pull off the scab, drain it, and clean it. I did what they said to do, though it doesn't seem possible that such an infection would cause Kalden such acute shortness of breath. Barry and I both thought, Oh, boy, here we go again with another bad case of pulmonary edema. We got out the P.E. [pulmonary edema] kit to be on the safe side. Barry checked Kalden's pulse, and it was 120; then he took the pulse of another Sherpa —108. So there wasn't too much difference. That softened our fears, and we put Kalden on oxygen. His pulse immediately dropped to 110. Once again we were able to avoid using the P.E. kit. We don't know yet what caused the Sherpa's illness. It could be pneumonia. We have given him the only shot of penicillin available up here, though Barry had some oral penicillin and Kalden seems to be responding quite well to a dose of that. . . . We have 17 full bottles of oxygen with us and we are using 3 of them for sleep tonight and will carry 8 to Camp 6 tomorrow. The wind is blowing 30 miles an hour tonight, and my feet are cold. I hope it quiets down by morning.

On the morning of May 21, Everest came up smiling and beaming. Lute and Barry and the others awoke at 6 A.M. Barry's oxygen had run out during the night, but Lute still had a little air left in his bottle. Both men had spent an uncomfortable night. Lute wrote in his diary:

I kept falling off my air mattress and freezing my rear end. Kalden still has those chest pains. I'm sure it's a case of carrying too much too high. He has simply had it! We are sending him back down with another Sherpa. A freezing wind blew all night, and at 5 A.M. it was —11 degrees. Please, God, give us just 36 more hours of good weather. Being cold all the time makes me wonder why we do these crazy things. It surely separates the men from the boys. Barry has been tremendous. I have been rather slow getting my work done, but once I start moving I am okay. There is a strong bond of comradeship between us. . . . The news from Katmandu that the newspapers are anxiously waiting for us to climb Everest takes the edge of *pleasure* off our task and replaces it with an edge of *duty*. This is disconcerting, because most people do not have the remotest idea of what we are forced to endure up here. . . . I have just put on my sleeping oxygen mask. It warms my toes. Oxygen suddenly makes the world seem less grim and cold and desolate, and more like a place where man can survive. I hope when we start on the final push to the summit I can prove strong. I don't want to crack. I am confident I will stand up under pressure here as well as I do anywhere. Man does not change basically. These rugged conditions only make a person less inhibited—but his basic nature does not change. If a man must come up to a place like the South Col to find his manhood, then he is escaping from life and himself. It is what he is inside that counts. *Be true to thyself* fits all occasions.

Upon reaching Camp 6, Lute and Barry had to dig the tents from the snow. It was 9 P.M. before they had the mess straightened out. To add to their

141

problems, Barry was feeling ill. Lute heated some soup for him, but it refused to stay down. "Try and get some sleep," Lute told him. Barry closed his eyes, but sleep would not come. "It feels like an attack of claustrophobia," Barry said. "I think I'm going mad. I can't breathe. The antibiotics—they are making me dizzy." Lute felt Barry's pulse. The heart was beating fast. Lute began to suspect something was organically wrong with his partner. He reached for the pulmonary edema kit, consisting of medical supplies for altitude sickness. If Barry had that dreaded high-altitude sickness, they were finished there and now. Barry pleaded for more time. He said, "Wait another hour. If I don't feel better by then, give me the shots." He leaned back again and tried to sleep. Lute opened his diary and began to write:

I said before leaving the States that I would be satisfied if I got to 25,000 feet on Everest, and here we are at 27,450 feet and going for broke. It will be a dirty shame if we are forced to quit after fighting so hard to reach this elevation. Barry's condition worries me. I pray to God he can get some sleep. We are trying to rest amid a conglomeration of clothing, oxygen gear, medicines, and photographic supplies. The wind continues to howl, and the air is killing, but the night is clear. Tomorrow should be ideal for climbing. I'm going to take a sleeping pill now and try to relax. Please, God, watch over us.

Down at Base Camp, Jim Whittaker stationed himself beside the radio, while at Camp 2 Maynard

Miller cocked an ear to his walkie-talkie. Earlier in the day, Norman Dyhrenfurth and several others climbed to 20,000 feet on Pumori and focused binoculars and telephoto lenses on the heights of Everest, hoping to locate the positions of the two summit teams. But they saw no movement—only rock, snow, and sky. Reluctantly they went back down to Base Camp to wait out the cold night. The fate of the climbers was in the hands of God now.

11

The View from Everest

The minute hand crawled around the face of Lute's wristwatch like a nightmare in slow motion. It was 2:30 A.M., May 22, and Lute and Barry did not talk much lying there in the eerie glow of the tent's butane stove at Camp 6. A word here and long gasps for air between, and then another word. In that manner the mind keeps quieter to do its own thinking.

Barry's breathing rose and fell unevenly. He was

in agony. Lute increased the flow of oxygen from 1 to 2 liters to ease Barry's breathing.

Lute could see Barry's white teeth, bare and alkali-dry in the glow of the stove; the red-eyed stare, the dried-out mouth open; the pain-racked body helpless against the weakness that clutched him with icy hands. Lute told himself that there had to be something crazy about any man who would purposely subject himself to such physical punishment. The longer you stayed up there, the crazier you got. It was like jungle fever. On and off. But every time it came, it stayed a little longer, until you died of it or it broke. Lute knew that they were both worn out, and they weren't going to get better until they got off the mountain. Any minute they could go loco.

Gradually the life-giving hiss of Barry's oxygen mask worked its magic. The eyelids fluttered shut, the chest stopped heaving, and he dropped off to sleep. Satisfied for the moment that his partner was going to be all right, Lute swallowed another sleeping pill and tried to doze off himself.

Wakefulness returned to Lute at 4:30 A.M., bringing him to his feet. He had chores to perform. He began preparing the two butane stoves to melt snow for hot soup. It was not unusual for them to lose as much as a cup of perspiration an hour at that elevation, and the soup would restore the body fluids they had lost during sleep. He had just started attaching a fresh gas cylinder to one of the stoves when

—whoo-sshh!—there was an explosion, followed by an instantaneous flash of orange flames. Suddenly one end of the tent was filled with fire. Lute had been leaning over the stove when it burst, and the stench of his smoldering beard brought Barry to his knees. In the next blinding instant the flames consumed Barry's plastic oxygen mask, singeing his eyebrows and whiskers. Puffs of gray smoke ballooned out of the tent. Panic gripped both men. *"Get out!"* Lute shouted. He tore furiously at the zippered entrance, with Barry right behind him. They moved so swiftly they nearly pitched themselves over the side of the ledge. A few feet farther, and they would have gone into Tibet.

Several moments later they crawled slowly back to the tent to assess the damage. Fortunately, there wasn't enough oxygen in the air at that altitude to keep the flames burning, and they had gone out quickly. Lute and Barry reassured themselves that nothing had been seriously harmed, and then sat back to recover from the shock. Silence hung heavy over the tent. Finally, Barry asked, "How did it happen?"

"Who knows!" replied Lute. "It happened."

"Lute, this is going to be one of our bad days. What a way to start to the summit."

"Yeah."

Barry stared at the blue sky outside. "Well," he said, hopefully, "at least we have the weather on our side." It was a clear day, not too windy, and almost perfect for a summit attempt.

Lute said, "I hope the wind is as good to us up at the summit."

To avoid weakening and exhausting themselves more than they already had, they prepared very slowly to leave. Barry's spirits seemed to be perking up. He said he was feeling stronger. He was regaining his self-confidence.

Lute went back to firing up the butane stove. This time there was no explosion. He brewed hot soup and adjusted the vital oxygen sets they would be carrying to the summit. At 8 A.M., they were ready to leave. They fastened their crampons, pulled outer windproof jackets over their down clothing, put on their heavy mittens, and stepped out into the cold air. The sun shone and Lute squinted into its glare at the ridge above them. What he saw was a thin, clean knife edge cutting into the sky. That ribbon of white was going to be their route to the summit. Lute turned to Barry:

"We're off."

"I'll make it," Barry vowed. "I'll make it even if I have to crawl on my hands and knees."

For the first half-hour Barry led the way, kicking steps in the soft snow that sloped toward the southeast ridge. His pace was slower than Lute's, however, and in due time Lute went to the head of the rope. Sometimes he followed the route's knife-edged crest, sometimes he sought firmer footing on lower snow. The sun was well up its arc in the sky now, and the mountain gleamed so brightly that it would have struck them blind if they had not worn goggles. They plodded silently on for another hour. And another. Their feet at every step broke through the thin crust into deep snow, their hearts pounded, their lungs felt scorched. The freezing bite of the wind stiffened clothing and pinched fingers beneath their mittens. Half-suffocated, Lute was forced to stop between each step and suck the raw, bitter air of his oxygen flow. After all, it wasn't the same as breathing clean, sea-level air. He averaged six gulps of air for every step, but this meager supply of thin air gave him only a fraction of the oxygen his parched lungs demanded. Now the ridge steepened into a great snowface, leading to the South Summit. Only faint vestiges of the footprints that Whittaker and Gombu had made three weeks before remained in the smooth whiteness, and Lute and Barry had to kick their own steps as they wound their way sky-ward. Seconds blurred into minutes, and minutes into eternity.

At 11 A.M., they stood at the top of the south-east ridge overlooking the 10,000-foot drop of the Kangshung Face into Tibet. There Barry switched positions with Lute and broke trail for the next 400 feet over another knife-edge of hard snow. Their pace grew slower. One foot forward, then the other.

One foot. The other. Every few minutes a blast of cold wind would hit them, and they would have to fight to keep their balance. On their left, a steep half-mile below, was the South Col; on their right, the awesome Kangshung Face. After several more gasping steps, they stopped. Now Lute took over the lead once more and resumed breaking trail. Dead ahead was their first major goal, the South Summit, towering another 500 vertical feet above them. The South Summit was only 278 feet from the Main Summit! Lute's hopes lifted. In a technical sense the route was not particularly difficult. There was always a place for the next stance or hold; it was an endurance contest now.

The battle went on. Two more hours. Two hundred more forbidding feet. On a rocky outcrop they paused long enough to eat the only food they would consume all day: a quarter of a candy bar apiece. After 10 minutes they were on the way again. They inched along a section where the footing was frightfully dangerous. There were rock outcrops on the left, and steep snow on the right. The slope tilted at a 45-degree angle. The tempo continued to lessen. Their rest periods grew longer.

Two hundred and fifty feet below the South Summit, Barry's first cylinder of oxygen ran out. Lute's was close to exhaustion, too. They sat down on a small ledge and changed bottles. They got up and started moving again on legs as unsteady as rubber. Lute remained in the lead. He had taken only a

149

couple of steps when suddenly there was a quick movement as Barry stumbled over one of the discarded empty oxygen bottles and flew off into space. He instinctively twisted in mid-air, hit the slope face-down, and somehow managed to claw at the snow with his hands and feet and stop himself. Lute was on his knees alongside Barry in a flash, grabbing him with his right hand and holding on for dear life. Carefully, a little at a time, they inched themselves back onto the ledge. There they lay, panting. Lute finally spoke first: "Boy, that could have been it." Barry only nodded. He was still trembling. Only split-second reflexes had prevented them from plunging into Tibet.

They finally stood again, adjusted their packs, and pushed on. Barry's bones ached. He felt spent, dull. He was having a bad day. And to have it on a day when so much was at stake! Barry chastened himself: "Every climber has these days, but I always dreamed of being *up* for this big one!" He felt miserable—but he wouldn't quit. He stumbled, he slipped, he rested at frequent intervals. He called upon every ounce of physical reserve to stay upright.

Now they had reached an elevation where each step required minutes of rest. They crossed hard, steep snow. Lute chopped steps until he thought his arm would drop off. The ideal route to the South Summit would have been the most direct one, Lute told himself, but Everest is not constructed to a man's specifications, so there had to be a lot of trial

and error: to the right, to the left, back again, up
again; continuous step-cutting—pausing for breath
—forging ahead a foot at a time—slowly—slowly.
One step—six long breaths—another step—another
six breaths. An hour passed. Another 30 minutes.
Then—

At 2 P.M., under a piercingly blue sky, they were
standing on the southern threshold of Everest's
Main Summit. They just stood there, too tired to
move. Above them loomed the giant peak of the
summit pyramid. With any luck they would be on
top in another hour. Their goal was close now, very
close, and yet it appeared to them almost as a second
whole mountain resting on top of the mountain
they had already climbed. Their vantage point was
already 500 feet higher than any other mountain on
earth! Lute peered up at the true and final summit
rising above them in craggy, snow-swept grandeur.
He had memorized the view a hundred times from
maps and photographs, but now it loomed steeper,
closer, more forbidding than he had imagined.

The agonizing journey continued. Three steps
and stop; three steps and stop. Each step, each slightest movement, was an enormous effort. Numbness
spread through their bodies. The roaring tide of air
grew ever stronger, the cold deeper. Gusts up to 70
miles an hour lashed at them, all but battering them
to their knees. They groped, they floundered, they
continued to hack their way upward. Sometimes
they were conscious of their hunger and fatigue,

sometimes only of growing numbness. Lute suddenly found himself gawking with dismay at a 20-foot vertical wall of rotten snow. It designated their jumping-off point for the Main Summit. He began moving due west, down a slight slope. He suddenly stopped, did a double take. Wait, that couldn't be the right way. "The vertical pitch has me spooked," he told himself. Lute turned and marched off down the left side. He had gone about 75 feet when he looked back over his shoulder and saw Barry motioning wildly at him. It was impossible to be heard clearly through their oxygen masks, but it was plain to tell by Barry's gestures that he thought his partner had cracked up and was going to end it right there. Realizing his error of direction, Lute made a fast pivot and ground his way back to the South Summit to start over again.

Lute made another check of his bearings. The last several hundred feet of Everest soared into space. The massive thrust of rock and ice seemed like a fang clamped against the blue-black sky. The sight of it chilled Lute's blood. He pushed into the lead once more, and his ax rose and fell methodically. The soft crunch of metal striking snow was the only sound in an immensity of stillness. All at once Lute was faced with the most formidable obstacle on the ridge: a 15-foot vertical cliff of rock. Jim Whittaker had warned them about it. To the left was space, to the right was a cornice—and more space. The rock wall itself was smooth and provided no place to get a hold. About the only alternative was a narrow crack running up the full height of the cliff between the cornice and the rock. Lute studied the problem and made his decision. He wedged himself into the crack as far as he could go, and, straining and clawing his way upward, worked his way to the top by climbing the rock itself rather than trusting the cornice and bad snow. Once he got a hand over the rim of the cliff and wiggled himself onto the level top, he belayed the rope. Barry followed up after him, and the final barrier in Everest's defenses had been hurdled.

It had been a grim struggle, but now the final minutes took the form and texture of a dream. They no longer needed to cut steps, but cramponed up the slope. The ridge rose in a series of white hummocks and curved to the right. They'd no sooner get over one hummock than another would pop up. Then another and another. Always farther; always higher. Fatigue was rapidly overtaking them, and they kept going on sheer nerve alone. The wind howled, and it was all they could do to stay to the left of the overhanging edge of the cornice on the right. Lute riveted his attention to his feet: lifting—placing—lifting—placing. Behind him, Barry was making the same supreme effort. They were putting everything they had into the final drive.

Lute was ahead of Barry by about 75 feet, and it finally dawned on him that the long ridge they were climbing reached the peak of its pyramid just beyond; after that it dropped sharply away. He then caught sight of a narrow snow ridge culminating in a distinct summit. There IT was: a white crest in the sky to which the American flag had been added. Lute spun around and gave the victory signal to Barry.

The summit of Everest had been sighted.

What was Lute thinking at that moment? The answer can be found in his diary:

Just then I came to a chest-high rise in the snow. I could see just over it, and my eyes caught a glimpse of the most beautiful sight I've ever seen—Old Glory. And seeing that great big wonderful flag whipping and crackling in the strong wind, its ends tattered after being there three weeks, I was reminded of the famous Iwo Jima flag-raising scene. Whittaker had done his job well.

It was 3:15 P.M. when the two men dragged themselves onto earth's ultimate pinnacle. It is foolish to speculate as to which of them was in the lead, which one can be classified as the *second* American in history to reach the top, because Lute waited for Barry to catch up with him, and then arm in arm they went over the top together. They were *together* in victory. Together, grinning through tears and goggles, wringing hands, thumping each other until forced to stop for lack of breath.

Men worship God in various way. It seemed to Lute at that moment, as he stood there on earth's crest, that he was truly worshiping God. Everything around him seemed somehow to be a miracle, a miracle gratefully accepted and explainable by the presence of Him. Silently and automatically Lute and Barry dropped to their knees in gratitude.

Then they went to work, for they were in a photographer's heaven. From where they stood the whole world fell away from them. They shut off their tanks to preserve what little oxygen was left and brought out their cameras. For the next 45 minutes they took pictures from all sides of the summit, until presently their hands fumbled and their movements became unsure. Then they stowed the cameras, replaced their masks and turned the oxygen back on again, giving themselves a flow of only 1 liter per minute. Lute patted his pack happily. It now contained the first motion pictures ever shot from the top of Everest.

Throughout the photographing, Lute and Barry kept thinking the same thing: Where were Willi Unsoeld and Tom Hornbein? The four of them were to have met on top at 3 P.M. It was now almost 4 P.M. and still there was no sign of them. They scanned the mountain hoping to catch a glimpse of Willi and Tom coming up, but their straining eyes saw nothing. The grim West Ridge was empty.

From the time Lute left the United States he had intended to leave a memento on the summit to commemorate his being there. Now he reached into his pack and pulled out his New Testament. He went over and placed it at the base of the flagpole. Somehow it seemed to Lute almost a sacrilege to leave that beautiful book up there. He looked down at it for a long moment with mixed emotions, then turned and stared down the West Ridge again for some sign, some possible hint, of the fate of Willi and Tom. But still he saw only snow and rock—height and depth—space and stillness. The absence of his two lost friends seemed to make up his mind for him, and in a gesture of finality he reached down and picked up the New Testament and put it back into his pack. He said out loud, "We're going to need this more than Everest does." That's all he said, and then he and Barry started down off the summit.

Their descent was now a dangerous race against time, exhaustion, and a rapidly dwindling oxygen supply. It was also a foot race in slow motion, for the route was perilous.

Down the ridge they groped. Down the vertical cliff. Down more ridge, on and on along the white twisting ribbon between the gulfs of space. Their pace grew slower, in the certain knowledge that the slightest misstep would plunge them both from the mountainside. The wind lashed at them, and the cold gnawed at their bones. And always there was the pressure of time, pushing them on to the very limits of physical endurance. Fearful that they could not survive if darkness overcame them, they continued down, on the verge of collapse. The killing wind and the blackness of night was all around them, and Lute was having trouble seeing. His right eye had taken a severe battering from the weather for several days now and was completely shut. His left eye, burned by the explosion of the butane stove, was a mere slit and he could barely see in front of him.

12

West Ridge: Point of No Return

On the West Ridge of Everest, three or possibly four miles from Lute and Barry, but hours and hours separated in time, the mountain was offering an unconquered face to Tom Hornbein and Willi Unsoeld. This was an ambitious venture, the American expedition's effort to place four men on the summit at the same time. The West Ridge had stood the investigation of more than a half-century of reconnaissance. It was believed to be unclimbable. Willi and Tom, toiling up that face, were leaving tracks in snow where man had never been before. This was an epic effort aimed at the summit and a descent via the South Col. Every step they took carried them farther along the point of no return. They *had* to reach the summit to survive, for there was no turning back down the route they traversed.

Theirs was probably the most drama-packed experience of the American expedition—a carefully planned long-shot venture that must end in victory or in death. They had to go up and over. There was no other way off the mountain for them.

Since 6:50 A.M., Tom and Willi had been creeping closer and closer to that point on the mountain where there was no turning back. They were investing all the skill and strength in them to tame this side of the mountain. By midafternoon the freezing currents had begun to batter the attackers. The higher they climbed, the slower the pace grew. Throughout the ascent Willi was in the lead breaking trail. He and Tom performed brilliantly together; over the years they had climbed many times together, and in pace, timing, and coordination they were the perfect team. It had been a long-cherished dream of theirs to climb Everest together.

At 3 P.M., they stood on a little square of rock 800 feet below the summit. They both knew that if they didn't continue forcing the pace, darkness would trap them. The worst of the climb was still in front of them, involving tests on difficult rock. They made their way over the intermittent rock and snow of the North Face, up a gully, up a finger, and finally onto a rock outcrop. At that point they paused long enough to make radio contact with Jim Whittaker down at Base Camp.

"Jim, we've lost our bearings," Willi said.

"Describe your approximate location," Whittaker said.

"I guess you could say it's the point of no return. We can see lots of gray rock above us, but can't see the summit."

"You should reconsider this carefully. I don't like the sound of your situation. You must always leave yourselves an escape route."

"We'll check with you again in about an hour and let you know what progress we are making. In the meantime we'll consider the possibility of retreat."

But both Willi and Tom knew they would never turn back. Using a rappel, the roping-down technique, would have been the normal method of descent, but that was now out of the question because the rock wall they had just come up had no projecting points on which to fasten rope. They had cut themselves off from the world below.

Willi and Tom felt much better after talking to Whittaker. The very act of communicating with someone from the world of the living had deeply moved them. Nine hours of steady, uphill slogging had made them extremely emotional. They had been pushing themselves so brutally there hadn't even been time for taking pictures.

Daylight was still on their side when they radioed Whittaker a second time to tell him that they had decided to try for the summit.

"We haven't gone crazy, Jim," Willi assured him. "We have talked it over very carefully, and we will not be turning back. You can help us. We must know everything you can tell us about the summit's configuration."

Whittaker told Willi everything he could remember, but no part of his description fitted their present position. He advised them to look for snow at the top, but from where they stood they could see only solid rock.

"Don't worry, Jim, we'll figure it out."

Willi and Tom pushed off once more toward the peak. They found the gray rock more to their liking now, and they seemed to grow stronger with every step. They still moved cautiously, however, inching along as men might travel through a mine field—half-hesitant, half-defiant.

They spent another hour laboring to the roof of a long snow slope. Then they angled up snow-powdered slabs that grew sharper and sharper. At 4:30 P.M., they stood near the top of the North Face (28,400 feet). Now Everest began to look within their reach. Their oxygen supply was ample, they had enough physical energy—and daylight had not yet failed them.

Their most favorable line of attack was a traverse back to the West Ridge, where they could get onto snow. They changed their course diagonally.

The wind really whipped at them now as Everest launched a nerve-racking, screaming gale.

After stopping briefly to eat a fast lunch of kippered snacks, the first food they had had since early breakfast, they resumed climbing. There was no talk as they climbed, for speech was impossible through the masks they wore. With the North Face and the miles of Tibet facing them on the left, and the deep white chasm of the Western Cwm far below on the right, they crept steadily on course in the direction of a sheer knife-edge of rock that grew in size before their eyes. Al Auten had described the deafening roar of Everest's high winds as sounding like a freight train crashing over rocks, but now that Willi was closer to it, he decided there was something more haunting about nature's melody. He compared it to the sound of ghostly fingers playing over the lower register of an organ's keyboard. It was a reverberation and a rumble, this voice of Everest that spoke to them.

As the later afternoon wore itself out and they drew closer to the summit, Willi and Tom could see the ridges converging from north and south on a little crown of snow above them. Tom kept telling himself that it couldn't be the summit because it was too close. He was sure that the crest was still off in space somewhere. But he felt that they were getting close.

Back at the knife-edge of rock, before working their way along its steep flank, they had stopped to

162

remove their steel crampons and overboots. From there they inched up one at a time for a distance of four rope lengths, each securing the other with rope. Having passed the rock, they were again on snow, and there they put on their boots and crampons again. The wind beat at them unmercifully now. They were near the top and exposed to all its fury.

Willi was moving very slowly. He had almost reached the end of his strength. They paused briefly to rest on the white slope. They went on again. Another brief rest. Then on again. They were near the final limits of physical endurance. But they had one more reservoir to tap: that deep inner strength that is resident in man, waiting to be called upon. It was nearly 6 P.M. now, and they were three hours overdue getting to the summit. Two hundred feet still stood between them and the top, at least another half hour's climb, and their margin of daylight for descent was running low.

Willi was breaking trail and his progress was no more than a crawl. It was incredible that a wind could blow so fiercely and so hard. It was a solid wind. It resisted their progress like a granite wall. Those last few feet were suddenly within their grasp. Willi stopped, coiled the rope, and stood their holding up his fist for Tom to see. Tom looked up and there IT was; 40 feet beyond Willi was the American flag. It shone brightly in the slanting rays and flapped wildly in the wind. It was wrapped around the picket and slightly frayed at the edges. *There* was the top of

163

Everest! Tom moved up alongside Willie, and they threw their arms around each other, engaging in a moment of mutual backslapping. No words were spoken. They were speechless, their emotions scraped raw by the climb.

The view of the tip of Everest from the west is more dramatic than the one from the south. It is not a final hump in a series of humps, but an entity in itself—a spearpoint to the sky. There, after more than 11 hours of punishment, Willi and Tom, arm in arm, marched those last few feet. At 6:15 P.M., they stood on top of Everest—the second team of Americans to do so within three hours! They represented the fifth and sixth members of the 1963 American Everest Expedition to get to the summit —and the first two men in history to get there via a route other than the South Col. Theirs would go down in mountaineering annals as one of the gigantic firsts.

As the sun began to escape behind the western ranges, two half-frozen men allocated the next 15 minutes to taking photographs of the breathless view: the sinking sunset, Makalu, Lhotse, and the valley. They left several mementos, including a crucifix wrapped inside Gombu's friendship scarf, and two prayer flags given to Willi by Sherpa Ang Dorje. They performed their duties in silence. The thoughts they had concerned the brotherhood of the moment and how closely the ascent had brought them together. (Willi said later: "It was a testimony to interpersonal relations rather than overcoming a great mountain.") Just as they finished readying themselves for the vital descent, they paused and gave thanks for the privilege that had been granted them, and for the necessary strength that had been provided to complete this climb.

In the deepening cold and grayness of the hour, they started down. About 50 feet below the summit, they stopped at a small patch of gravel and set up their walkie-talkie. The time was 6:33 P.M. They couldn't raise Base Camp, but they did reach Maynard Miller, at Camp 2. Static filled the air, making communication almost unintelligible, but they got across the point that they had been to the summit and were now on their way back down via the Col route. Maynard wanted to know about Jerstad and Bishop. "Have you seen any sign of them? There's been no word from them for several days."

"We saw fresh tracks on the summit," Willi replied, "so they must have been there." Willi signed off with a quotation from Robert Frost: "I have promises to keep / And miles to go before I sleep." Brief as radio contact had been, it marked the very first time that man had communicated from the top of Everest with the world below.

If it strained belief that Unsoeld and Hornbein had successfully climbed Everest from the West Ridge side, few bettors would have taken 100-to-1 odds on their chances of traversing the Col route and returning to Base Camp alive.

165

Down they moved—carefully, probingly—following the footprints of Jerstad and Bishop whenever they could be found. They could see down the ridge only as far as the South Summit. Nowhere was there any movement on that sharp icy thorn. Shouting was out of the question, for all sound was blocked off by the subpeak. The sun dropped out of sight. Twilight darkened into dusk, then dusk into night, and, except for a dim flashlight, it was in near blackness that they crawled up the 30 feet to the South Summit. It took them 45 minutes to traverse this distance.

Down Hillary's Chimney (a steep, narrow cleft in a rock wall) they crept, weaving, stumbling, slipping, resting when exhaustion forced them to stop. Then down again, lowering themselves ever so carefully down the steep icy route—always down. They were conscious of the thin air and the fight for breath, and of the growing numbness in hands and feet. Periodically they experienced the high-altitude illusion that they heard voices. Below them, what they thought were solid landmarks appeared and vanished like mirages time and time again. Breaking trail on the way up had been Willi's chore; leading them down was Tom's responsibility.

A near crisis broke out below Hillary's Chimney. Tom had stopped and motioned furiously to Willi. At first, Willi thought Tom had punctured the bladder of his oxygen mask, but closer inspection revealed that he had banged the bottle on a rock while sliding down a small pitch, causing a loud hissing of wasted air. It turned out to be only a minor problem, one that was easily remedied by adjusting the regulator and stopping the leak before much oxygen had escaped.

Part of the way down they had been able to follow Lute's and Barry's tracks, but after a while they lost them in some rocks. They stood in the snow momentarily, debating the possibility of bivouacking, and decided it would be better to go on. They cut down across the rocks to their left, on out into the middle of a snow slope. Sometimes the snow was good, sometimes it was soft. Sometimes it was so shallow that they struck rock after their axes had driven only a couple of inches. The wind hit them from behind and from the front, and the cold bit all the way to the bone. To add to their miseries, Willi's flashlight was dying. So they turned it off and traveled in blackness. It was necessary now to cut their 120-foot rope in half so that they could tie themselves much closer together.

They stumbled on for another hour before Willi stopped and sat down. He told Tom, "Maybe we had better stay here and take our chances with the night."

Tom said, "Turn on your flashlight once more. Let's see if there are any tracks below."

Even in the dim glow they were able to see the marks of a track just below them. Together they yodeled, hoping to attract attention. They thought they were above Camp 6, where Dave Dingman might hear them and come up and guide them to safety. Their calls brought faint shouts. They moved down faster now.

"It's Dingman!" Willie cried. "He hears us!"

Tom said, "Then we are near Camp 6."

His voice strained with irritation, Willi asked, "But why doesn't he show a light? He could show us where the lousy camp is if he would just flash a light!"

Willi and Tom grew confused. They kept flashing their own dim light but received no response. Their descent once more was slowed to a groping, stumbling crawl. It was 8 P.M. . . . 9 P.M. . . . 9:30 P.M. . . . 9:45 P.M. Now they heard another shout from below.

Willi said, "It sounds like a Sherpa."

They cupped their ears to listen again.

Tom said, "Sounds more like Dingman."

"Wait a minute," Willi said, "there it is again."

Using his hands for a megaphone, Tom shouted, *"Is that you, Dingman?"*

There was no answer. Tom's voice had been lost in the wind. Willi tried next: "HELLOOOO! HELLOOOO! HELLOOOOO!" Another long period of silence elapsed. "Why doesn't he flash a light?" Willi muttered.

Suddenly another yell floated up from below. Tom said, "Hear that? They're still there."

"Come on," Willi said, "let's go!"

168

They went down across the endless ridge. In their fuzzy state of mind, they were wondering if real voices had called to them from below. They heard voices again:

"This way—come on."

Through the haze below, they sensed what seemed to be a speck—two specks—and this time it was no illusion. There *were* two figures, standing there in the snow, waiting. Two familiar figures. But the darkness was so thick and overpowering that when Tom put out a hand and touched the first figure he came to, he could not identify him.

"Is that you, Dingman?" he asked.

"No," the voice answered, "it's Lute. Lute and Barry."

Willi arrived behind Tom and dropped wearily into the snow. While it was a relief to be with old friends again, both Willi and Tom felt a sharp prick of disappointment. They had thought the voices they had heard represented tents, sleeping bags, and a measure of rest. Lute and Barry were still some 850 feet above the haven of Camp 6. Incidentally, here was where the unforeseeable luck of the butane stove's explosion had played its role: Had it not been for that delay in starting for the summit, Lute and Barry would have been back to Camp 6 at the time Willi and Tom began shouting. Inside a tent, at such a distance, the yelling would have been drowned out in the roaring wind. There is providence in all things, and there on Everest it was manifested.

Tom said, "Let's go. This is no place to spend a night."

Conferences were unnecessary—get down!

All vestiges of Lute's and Barry's morning footprints were lost in the night; all contact with Base Camp was cut off. They were marooned on a frozen perch high in the sky. Their task seemed impossible. Yet an attempt had to be made. Lute's diary reveals the full drama and horror of those hours:

With our oxygen exhausted, with Willi's fading flashlight our sole illumination, with my eyes swollen nearly shut, with our strength so spent we could barely stand—we felt our way along. We were so fuzzy-headed from fatigue and lack of air we were willing to walk through hell to get to Camp 6. Tom and Willi, fresher and more alert, took charge, and they verbally whipped us into going on, pushing me and pulling Barry when we began to falter. We were dead on our feet. On and on. Resting. Tom cracking the whip to keep us upright. Willi scolding Barry into wakefulness: "Anybody can walk a hundred feet! Anybody! No matter how tired you are, keep going." We covered only 300 feet in the next two hours. Camp 6, wherever it was, was still far below.

Down that somber ridge the four climbers staggered through the bleakness. Men against the mountain. Exhausted men plumbed to depths of weariness that are revealed to few persons. They reached deeper and deeper into their hidden store of endurance and found it seemingly inexhaustible. They kept on their feet—long after they should have stretched in the frozen snow to die. They proved to themselves how really tough and tenacious the desire to live can be. But there comes a point when man reaches the last limit of endurance.

At 12:30 A.M., they reached the limit. They would have to take their chances at 28,200 feet on Everest.

13

Miracle in the Sky

It was 12:30 A.M. and pitch dark. They were trapped. Face to face with a usually lethal, high Himalayan ordeal: a night in the open. No one had ever survived an overnight bivouac above 26,000 feet. There was a theory that no one could survive. They would test it now and establish its falsity—or its truth.

Thoughts of spending the next six hours above 28,000 feet left Lute raw and frayed. Somehow the whole sequence of horrible events seemed unreal, as though it was happening to someone in a storybook. Only this was no fantasy. This was for real. There was sky, there was snow and wind and cold; there was also the growing numbness in his hands and feet, creeping like a slow paralysis through the body. Sleep was the great hunger; but Lute knew he must not give in to it lest he freeze to death. He must remain awake and hoard the warmth in his body by moving his toes and fingers.

They had found an outcropping of rock on the snow of the ridge and paired off. Lute and Barry bedded down in the snow, Willi and Tom on the rock. As the temperature dropped to −18, the four men thumped and rubbed themselves, knocked their feet together, held their hands under their armpits—anything—to keep the blood circulating.

The hours that followed were hardening knots in the strands of time. Lute managed to keep moving, but while one part of him fought for the spark of life, another part seemed to be watching from nearby. *You can't go on*, the querulous small voice insisted. *This is habit carrying on, not you. You and your friends might as well give up—you don't have a chance.* But it is not in a man to give up; something animal and automatic keeps him going. Lute refused to quit, although he was certain that frostbite would take his feet. By this time all of the men were suffering from the nip of frostbite. Tom began to complain of the pain in his feet. The thought of one's limbs being transformed into inhuman chunks of ice is not a pleasant one. There was no panic, but rather a serenity that quiets fear, an inner strength which reckons with the situation and makes the proper decision. Willi insisted that Tom remove his boots and socks.

Tom managed to struggle out of his footwear, and then Willi tried a method familiar to all polar travelers. He unbuttoned his shirt, lifted his woolen undergarments, and selflessly let his partner slip his feet against the warmth of his bare stomach. He then began working the flesh gently with his hands, moving the blood back into circulation. No greater code could a man have to abide by and to live with than the gesture Willi made that night. He lay there for several hours, massaging Tom's feet.

Lute knew he was in good company. If anybody could survive this night, the four of them could. But he also knew that if he were to survive he'd have to take control of his emotions and dwell only on those thoughts that would strengthen his confidence. A discordant mind, dark with despair and confusion, would finish him off as thoroughly as the freezing wind. Therefore he searched for sources of replenishment. He drew from what he knew about the experience of every man who had ever challenged Everest. Mallory and Andrew Irvine had died on Everest, and their bodies never were found. Had they known they were going to die? What sort of battle had they put up? Had they huddled against the cold as fiercely as Lute and Barry and Tom and

Willi were huddling? Had they been afraid of death? Lute could not fight off the ominous feeling that their chances of surviving were growing slimmer by the hour. He thought, *We should have been dead hours ago. How much longer can we hold out?* He had gone without oxygen for nearly ten hours, and in spite of all his efforts to think positively, he had to admit to himself that the prospects of the four of them living through the night appeared very small.

For 27 years Lute had lived in the world of civilization, but he was now seeing it through eyes tempered by fire. From the highest point on earth one more easily realizes what wonders lie below, the pleasantness of daily luxuries: fresh air—green fields —the smell of ripe clover—the sweet taste of well water—flowers in bloom. Lute had accepted these gifts of God to man, and not known what was his until they began slipping away on Everest.

As the night wore on, Lute felt himself sinking. He had faced death before, but not like this, defense-less. Death was a stranger sitting on a nearby ledge, waiting, biding his time. The survival record in Lute's mind began to spin again, playing a monoto-nous single note. It was still spinning when drowsi-ness overcame him. He lived in a dreamful, fretting state of facts, real and imaginary. Then, in flashes, came wakefulness; superalert wakefulness, long-overdue wakefulness, the feeling of having slept for days.

Lute looked at his watch. It was 2:30 A.M. He

had been alive one more hour. He went back to wiggling his toes again. He kept it up until a sense of feeling crept back into them. He wondered about Willi and Tom. There had been very little talk. Willi was still massaging Tom's feet. Barry had dozed off. His breathing was irregular. He was having a hard time. A stealthy languor crept across Lute's chest and flowed down into his legs. His wrists ached, and his fingers were quite dead to the touch.

Meanwhile, down at Base Camp, tension mounted. Jim Whittaker kept watch by the radio. For seven hours there had been only silence. His last contact was at 6:33 P.M. —the whoop of triumph from Tom and Willi at the top—but what about Lute and Barry? What was their fate? No one knew; the battery in Lute's walkie-talkie had run out of juice long ago.

Through that terrible night the men at Base Camp beat a path to the radio shack.

"Any word yet?"

"What's going on up there?"

"Isn't their radio working?"

They had already lost Jake Breitenbach. Was Everest going to make it five? They had made the effort. What was the price?

High above them, four men were enduring their worst hours on earth. The seconds sweated lazily off the face of time. The men remained silent. There was no oxygen, but the masks protected their faces from the cold and they kept them on. Everest had punished them unmercifully; yet, in that ultimate crisis when it had them cornered, it showed heart. Lute couldn't believe it was really happening. It had to be a wild dream. But it was true: that vicious wind had mysteriously stopped—for the first time in 93 straight nights it did not rip and tear like a mighty organ. It was a big break. In restrospect, an enormous break. A genuine miracle. There was only an occasional gust, then stillness and blackness and the frozen stars. Why, Lute asked himself, should the wind stop blowing on the one night they were trapped outside? He knew the answer: *Somebody up there wants us alive.*

Lute fought hard against the growing desire to close his eyes, because in sleep his inert body would grow even colder. He waited—he huddled—he hugged himself—he shivered. The only parts of him that did not feel the cold were his fingers and feet, which were numb. All sensation had gone from them. The climb down from the summit had kept his heart pumping blood to the surface of his body and to all the extremities. But the instant he stopped moving, the action of the pump slowed down. The cold of space smote him.

Now he had to keep his hands and feet moving to pump life-giving blood to the surface. The instant he stopped it ebbed away and sank down into the recesses of his body. The extremities were the first to

177

feel its absence. His wet feet froze the faster, and his fingers through his gloves numbed the faster. It was incredible, the speed with which his feet and fingers froze. They seemed remote from his body and from him. When he tried to pull the zipper on his down jacket, he had to look and see whether or not he had hold of it. He spent the entire night with the jacket unzipped. The sensory nerves were pretty well numbed, and his body was ill-connected. He felt like a puppet on a string—with no one to pull the string and make him move.

Lute knew he had never experienced such deep misery. He looked at his watch. Three o'clock. Two more hours of frozen immobility before sunup. Through bloodshot eyes the blurred silhouettes of neighboring peaks faintly took form: range upon range of towering shadows, appearing now as no more than inky outlines; so unnatural that he seemed to be viewing them not from the planet earth at all, but from a fantastic island in the sky. An island with four specks on it that were men alone. His experience was reaching beyond fear—or even fear of fear. Sometime, years away, the sun would come up. He would wait.

A few hours earlier he had wanted desperately to get all the way down to warmer weather in the lowlands. Now he would gladly settle for the warmth of Camp 6, that wonderful haven of flapping nylon. At times his mind seemed to float away from his body. Darkness, time, and the aching cold took the place of a mind in his skull. Periodically he dozed. The rest of the time he was a thinking animal.

Lute had many pertinent thoughts as he waited for dawn. He thought of the four of them reaching the summit in one day. Everest, the lodestone of the Himalayas, which had lured brave men to their deaths for nearly half a century. Had it fallen to the three American teams too easily? Would those daring mountaineers of another age have resented this mass assault? Probably not, for the grim guardian of earth's highest point accepted no man as visitor until he had been tried and tested by the severest punishment.

He thought about those 45 minutes he and Barry had spent at the summit. Originally he had intended to record in detail his emotions up there. But time was limited, and there were duties to perform. There had been no time up there for emotions and the reflections he had anticipated. Uppermost was the sensation he experienced when he slipped off his oxygen mask to take motion pictures. Breathing at that height had been a real problem and moving without oxygen down those sharp ridges a nightmare.

Lute knew his companions had similar discomforts. They were pooling pitiful resources—all four of them. That night, they all learned the true length of an hour, and found it to be only endless time.

Lute, at last, could fight off fatigue no longer and drowsed off into half-wakeful impressions. Suddenly, he was imagining himself viewing his own stiff body. He thought how men would view that death. He saw the outcrop of rock and the four of them lying motionless in the snow. In his vision he was no longer part of himself. He was disembodied. He was part of infinite nothingness. Pain, cold, misery— what were they? They had nothing to do with the real life of Lute. They were false—they were a lie— he was true.

"Lute! Wake up!"

Gingerly, Lute opened first one eye and then the other, and peered around him. He was still alive. The others were alive. A magnificent fireball of sun was wedging itself from its night's sleep, painting Everest with liquid gold. No oil portrait could ever show it as it looked to Lute then. What a world. And what a sun. It was warm. It was day. It was a new day of life.

Lute raised his face to the sky in a gesture of gratitude.

He moved his arms. He looked down at his hands to locate them, and found them hanging there on the ends of his arms, frozen like tree branches in winter. It struck him as curious that he should have to use his eyes in order to find out where his hands were. Everyone was eager to get started. The inventory of physical damage could come later. The night undoubtedly would cost them some toes and fingers; but that was a small price to pay when they considered the stakes they had been gambling with for the last six hours. They had to get *home*, to Base Camp, and what a warm and friendly place it would be.

Willi and Tom went first, followed at an interval by Lute and Barry. The tracks that Lute and Barry had made on the way up now served as a trail. They were walking again in a familiar world.

At Camp 6, Dave Dingman had stood outside the tent and swept the high white wilderness with his glasses from late afternoon until sundown. For hours he had stared into that world of space, and seen nothing. Occasionally he thought he heard voices, but it could have been only the wailing of the wind. Nima Dorje and Girmi Dorje were with him, and they had spent the previous day hopefully vigilant, positive that Lute and Barry had gotten to the summit. By 6 o'clock that evening, however, the two men had not returned. At 7 o'clock darkness began to fall, and the concern at Camp 6 developed into alarm. The batteries in the only flashlight they had were growing weaker, but every 15 minutes Dave stood outside making flashing signals. There was no response. About 9 o'clock he heard what he was sure was shouting. The shouts came from up on the ridge. He stirred Girmi from his sleeping bag.

"Can you hear voices, Girmi?"

The Sherpa shook his head. "No, Sahib, only wind."

Dave went back inside his tent and waited. Once again he thought he heard voices. Was it only his imagination? He cupped his hands and shouted into the darkness. It was useless. His sounds were lost in the wind. Then long silence.

An hour passed. Then—

"Wh-oo-oo . . ."

Dave sat up, perking his ears. That definitely was not the wind. That was a human voice. There— there it was again—

"Wh-oo-oo down there . . ."

Dave grabbed the flashlight, went outside, and started blinking it again. His efforts proved useless, as the light from the worn batteries barely penetrated the darkness. Dave went to Girmi's tent and said, "Get dressed, we're going up there and try to find them."

Dave was certain that the shouts had come from above Camp 6 and to the west. Despite the hour, 10 P.M., and the pitch blackness, they started in that direction, up and across the steep, loose snow-covered rock. Dave was sure that the shouts he had heard came from Lute and Barry, and that they had veered off the regular South Col route too far to the west to spot his flashlight signals. Girmi carried two bottles of oxygen, one for Lute and one for Barry, and he and Dave pushed through snow and darkness

The Stars and Stripes wave to Lute Jerstad as he nears the top of the pinnacle, May 22, 1963. Photo was taken by his partner, Barry Bishop.

Norman G. Dyhrenfurth, leader of the American Mount Everest
Expedition, at Base Camp on the Khumbu Glacier.

Jim Whittaker

Nawang Gombu

Lute Jerstad

Barry C. Bishop

Tom Hornbein

Willi Unsoeld

Sherpas combine to carry Willi Unsoeld down from Base Camp to a helicopter near Namche Bazar. Willi suffered such severe frostbite it was necessary to amputate his toes.

Gilbert Roberts, AMEE

Barry Bishop, frostbite victim, rests his damaged feet on the
way back to a hospital in Katmandu. His toes were already
turning black.

The Expedition members at Namche Bazar after the conquest of Mount Everest. Front row (left to right): Dr. William Siri, Norman G. Dyhrenfurth, Barry W. Prather, and Nawang Gombu. Middle: Dr. David L. Dingman, Barry C. Bishop, Dr. William F. Unsoeld, Dr. Thomas F. Hornbein, Luther G. Jerstad, and Richard Pownall. Back: Lt. Col. James O. M. Roberts, Dr. Gilbert Roberts, Dr. Maynard M. Miller, James W. Whittaker, Dr. James T. Lester, Jr., Allen C. Auten, Knut A. Solbakken, Dr. Richard M. Emerson, James Barry Corbet, and Daniel E. Doody. Members not shown are James R. Ullman and John E. Breitenbach.

Pownall has his beard trimmed by a Sherpa "barber" on the way back.

Jerstad receiving the coveted Hubbard Medal from President
John F. Kennedy.

for several hundred feet until they reached the area Dave was convinced the voices had come from. They found nothing. Dave tugged off his oxygen mask and shouted. Girmi shouted. They listened for an answer. They shouted together. They waited. The only answer was the muffled roar of the chilling wind. Reluctantly they turned around and went back down to Camp 6.

While the two Sherpas slept, Dave sat in his tent listening for calls that never came. He was still in a sitting position when he fell asleep at 3 A.M.

Dave managed to get an hour and a half of sleep, but at 5:30 that morning he and Girmi were back on the trail. Both men were fit, and prepared for what originally was to have been a summit attempt—the seventh and eighth members of the American expedition to reach the top—but their thoughts no longer rested on Everest's pinnacle. The character of their mission now was one of rescue—or the search for several dead bodies.

Dawn had come up cold and clear. All around Dave and Girmi, as far as the eye could see, their route was unbroken white, save for the heavy footprints that curved and twisted in a dark hairline up the slope. That dark hairline was the main route made by Lute and Barry the day before, the trail leading all the way to the top. Had they been up there under different circumstances they would have had an excellent chance of going all the way. But with their companions in trouble—or dead—it was

183

inconceivable to even think about the summit. They plunged on. The trail was faint. Wind-swept snow had filled many of the steps during the previous day. They had progressed about 300 feet uphill when Dave held up his hand in a signal to stop. Were his eyes deceiving him? The frozen moisture of his breathing had settled on his goggles, blurring his vision. He strained. He ripped off his mask for a clearer look. "Girmi," he said. "Up ahead there. Does that look like somebody in the snow?"

"Sahibs still alive!" cried Girmi. And then they were shouting at once. The snow came alive as two figures staggered slowly to their feet.

Dave yelled, "Wait there! We'll bring oxygen to you."

Dave was astounded. The nearer he drew to the two climbers, the more confused he became. Was he losing his mind? It finally dawned on him that it wasn't Lute and Barry he saw, but Willi and Tom.

"What are you guys doing on the *south* side of the mountain? Where did you come from?"

"The top of Everest," Tom said.

"What happened to Lute and Barry?"

"They're not far behind us. You'd better go on to them with the oxygen. Both are in bad shape. We can get down from here."

Dave and Girmi went on up the trail. A hundred feet farther on they stopped. Dave let out another war whoop. For the second time within minutes his shouting brought climbers to their feet.

When Lute stood up he could see movement and hear voices. His first thought was that this might be another dream. He could not be sure.

"Sit down, we'll be right there!" Dave yelled.

It was no dream this time. It was indeed the world advancing to meet them. Suddenly all the despair and suffering of the last 24 hours fell away, and the joy that only the lost or condemned know at being saved filled their hearts.

And then they all went home, back down to Camp 6, where Tom and Willi and Nima Dorje were waiting. Tears welled up in Lute and Barry when those two little orange tents came into view. In a half-whisper, Lute said, "I never thought anything could look so tremendous."

By some miracle, they were safe at last, but part of Lute would remain forever up there on that outcropping of rock. On the other hand, he was taking away something that he had not fully possessed before: appreciation of being alive, a newborn respect for man, and a humble set of values. Sometimes a man must travel to the edge of death to secure that inner peace which provides a richer personal life.

Later, in the warmth and safety of Nepal's valleys, Lute revealed some of his inner thoughts about the bivouac:

I had a glimpse of the world above in its despair, victory, and uncertainty. I knew that the world down

185

here would look different when I came back to it.
And yet that world certainly hasn't changed. It is I
who have probably been inverted in some manner.
An experience like Everest strengthens men to
understand themselves and their surroundings. Everest is simply one more way of understanding yourself.
It does not mean anything materially. To the man
who says: "Surely all things will be anticlimatic after
climbing Everest! What's left?" I can only say, "I am
sorry for you that you feel that way." We live in a
world where we seem to gather strength from credit
ratings and college degrees. We build tiny private
worlds in the mountains and on the seashores to
escape from the hustle and bustle of life. We dare
not trample on time and space, which society organizes, for then we are outside of society. Therefore, we
adapt our lives to a pattern, for in that patterned existence lies security and strength. Everest has sharpened those perceptions for me. Mountains are not
dreamlike places where men can forget life for a few
hours and then dejectedly return to their jobs. On
the contrary, mountains bring men back into contact
with the very essence of life. Life is found in the soul
of man, and there we are all wealthy. Almost everything which we understand in life has been accompanied by pain of one kind or another—physical or
spiritual. I have had a confrontation with time on
Everest, and it is not pleasant to view yourself under
such close scrutiny. The night the four of us were
forced to bivouac at 28,200 feet, nothing mattered
any more. A new idea of life had to be found through
a direct confrontation with ourselves. I cannot really
say how Willi, Tom, and Barry spent the entire
night, for we seldom spoke. Each man was wrapped
in thoughts which none of us probably will ever be

able to express adequately. Even when we did talk, we were in our own realms. We did not desert each other, yet each was alone. We felt each other's presence, but we did not feel. We saw each other, but could not see. We knew each of us was safe, yet we knew nothing. We had come to a void where we were nothing and everything at the same time. I must speak only for myself and my feelings, for my comrades' feelings are their own. Up there, I knew *who* and *what* I was. The things which we generally term unrealistic and fantastic became reality, because they had to do with the innate power of man's understanding. It is shocking to learn so much about yourself in such a short time. It was as if 20 years had been telescoped into a few fleeting minutes. I had reached the void of seeing man's insignificance, greatness, simplicity, and complexity all in one bundle. I could look down upon the trappings of my very being. I looked forward, not backward, and could see what lay ahead of me and was strengthened to understand life in entirely new contexts. I now view life differently from the way I did yesterday. I will view it still differently tomorrow. Man will always change if he is to go forward. The life that men find by intuition is a good life. They will find it nowhere except in themselves, and they must look for no answers in other men. That kind of truth will be wholly alien and strange even to the man who knows it, for it knows no limitations. What we have just discovered about our abilities to survive under such adverse conditions is that man's limits shall never be reached. Intellectual and physical curiosity will never end. In the mountains men can find strange strengths. There are perhaps 5,000 climbers technically more competent and physically stronger than

187

Everest Diary

I. Every man who has ever reached the summit of any high mountain will readily admit that it was more than brute strength that carried him there. Man makes his own breaks and follows them up with all his ingenuity, skill, strength, endurance—and luck. And so, the mountains provide men with experiences which each must weigh and interpret. The same is true for writing, painting, research, athletics —or adventure. The important thing is that men search themselves for the meaning the experience has for them personally.

14

Four Came Back

Writing in his diary within the safety of Camp 6's nylon tent, and looking occasionally at his bedraggled, gaunt, and pitiful companions, it was hard for Lute to remember in detail all that they had recently been through. The full impact of the experience would come later. In a matter-of-fact style, he wrote:

Yesterday we went to the summit of Everest. Barry and I left here at 8 A.M. Earlier, at 5 A.M., our butane stove blew up, singeing my beard, eyes, and tongue. It was terrifying for a short time not knowing if we would get out. We got to the South Summit at 2 P.M., very beat. Barry was extremely tired and having trouble. We reached the Main Summit at 3:15 P.M. almost out of oxygen. We turned off the tanks to take pictures. I had gone up there on only 2 liters, and didn't use any on the way down except to get up the steep pitch at the South Summit. At about 7:30 or 8 P.M. we heard shouts. Willi and Tom had come over the top and were heading down. We waited for them until after 10 P.M. at the base of the South Summit. It was dark, and I could not see. I was blind in one eye from freezing wind, and the other eye was blurry. We tried to get to Camp 6, but only negotiated the knife-edge ridge and there bivouacked at 12:30 A.M. All four of us had by that time been out of oxygen for hours. I had only breathed some in spurts since 3 P.M. Up there on that ledge it was −18 degrees and Barry, Willi, and I suffered frostbite. We spent the night at 28,000 feet without sleeping bags, oxygen, food, fuel, liquid, or shelter. We should all be dead. . . .

After inspecting the extent of their frostbite, the men were impatient to get moving. Every hour they spent at Camp 6 was one more hour before they got back to Base Camp and proper medical aid. They were going to get to Base all right. There was no question about that. But the route was slow and cruel. Together the five Americans and two Sherpas descended to the South Col, the Lhotse Face, the Western Cwm, Advance Base, and—at last—Base

Camp. They traveled for two full days in one long, painful march. At Camp 4, Bishop sat down and went through the laborious process of removing his crampons, overboots, boots, all the way down to his socks, and for the first time thoroughly examined his feet. They were still numb, and white as snow. They had not yet started to turn black, and it was still too early to determine the seriousness of the damage.

As wrung and drained as their bodies were, there was an inner elation in the men all the way to Base Camp. Morale was high, and well it should have been, for they were going home. They were returning to the wonderful world of warmth, of greenness, and of living people.

They entered Base Camp at 6:30 P.M. on a Friday. Their arrival brought comrades rushing out of tents in a montage of backslapping, clasping hands, laughter, and tears. Like a smoke signal, the news of the return of the little band of bone-thin climbers swept through camp.

For a few magical moments Jim Whittaker and Lute stood apart, looking at each other. Two kids from Puget Sound. Everest had reduced Lute to a mute, crippled form. His haggard face, scraggly beard, and swollen eyes offered a picture of decrepitude. Jim was filled with compassion at the sight of his friend. He had been through the same hell and knew how much Lute had suffered. Lute had to squint at Jim, because his eyes were no more than

191

mere slits. Seeing Lute like that, Jim succumbed to his paternal instincts. He went over to Lute and put his arms around him, in the manner of a father welcoming back a son who has been reported missing in action. They spoke no words, for talk was unnecessary. Tears ran down their cheeks, and they did not bother to wipe them.

The four tired survivors were filled with a sense of relief. Relief that there were no more summits on Everest to climb, no more steps to chop, no more oxygen masks to adjust, no more gales to buck, no more ridges to traverse—and no more giant peaks to taunt them. Victory was officially theirs now, victory over the grimmest of enemies. If relief was quickly followed by jubilation, this in turn was followed by humility and meditation. Perhaps it was this moment above all others that gave special meaning to their victory: that it was a common triumph in a common cause. The *team* had won, all 965 of them. The victory belonged not only to the six men who actually got to the summit, but to the entire contingent of Americans, Sherpas, and porters. It was a *team* effort in every sense of the word.

On the way down from the summit Barry Bishop's frozen feet had started thawing, and by the time they had reached Camp 3 he was in deep pain. Now, at Base Camp, he went to a bottle of Scotch he had been keeping for just such an occasion. He felt the need of a little revival to dull the excruciating pain. As a matter of truth, he felt he needed quite a bit of revival. Then he flopped out on his sleeping bag and slept the sleep of the just and innocent. Tomorrow he would be going home.

While the end of the dreary battle brought gigantic relief, it was not the time or the place to exhibit hilarity. Somehow it would have seemed sacrilegious to make a noisy show out of it with singing and dancing—there was one, Jake Breitenbach, who would never sing and dance again. On the night they returned to Base Camp, Lute wrote:

Coming down from Camp 2, Bishop, Dingman, and I stopped below the dump we had established in March and stared quietly at the collapsed, chaotic icefall where Jake lies buried. We just stood there, remembering that big lovable character with the wide grin and blond hair—sort of a private memorial service. While looking down on all that icy rubble, Barry said: "Well, Jake, we got that old summit for you." In all the times we went up and down the icefall I don't think we ever passed that spot where Jake is buried that we didn't think of him. My hands and feet are burning like fire now. The more frostbite thaws the more it hurts. The pain is hard to describe. It starts at the bottom of the foot and creeps right up through the body, like a red-hot poker. It hurts to place any weight on my feet. But my case is mild compared to Barry's and Willi's. Arrangements have been made for a helicopter to pick them up at Namche Bazar. We will ride on the backs of Sherpas from here to the village, a hike of about 18 miles. Hornbein is okay and can walk out under his own power. I'm going to try to get some sleep now. . . .

The expedition moved onto the trail bright and early the next morning. Four porters were assigned to each of the three crippled Americans. The Sherpas made a game out of it. A fierce rivalry sprang up between the four porters carrying Barry and the four in charge of toting Willi. They reached Namche Bazar in slightly under two days.

The helicopter had not yet arrived, but it was scheduled to reach the mountain village within the next 48 hours. Only Barry and Willi would take the chopper, while Lute, a less serious case, would stick with the marchers and continue to ride the Sherpas piggyback until such time as the medics said he could walk again.

Bishop awoke early on that first morning following the expedition's arrival at Namche Bazar, and, noting an overcast sky, predicted that the day would bring no helicopter. He went back to sleep. Twenty-five minutes later, however, the whir of chopper blades snapped him to attention. The copter had arrived, through murk and all.

An hour later Barry and Willi hobbled out to the waiting machine. They both needed the support of ski poles and Sherpas. As for Barry, talk had left him gradually during the final hour. He thought about his comrades staying behind. When he reached the helicopter door, he paused, "Well, fellas—" he said, and he took off his beaten-up ski cap, holding it in his right hand. He held up his left hand in a gesture of good-by. "Take care of yourselves—" The tears flooded his eyes then, and he rubbed at the corners. They channeled the deep grime of his face. He could not cry, for the muscles of his throat and chest were caught tight. And then he and Willi were gone—two faces pressed to the window until they were out of sight.

For Barry Bishop and Willi Unsoeld, the war against Everest was history.

15

Farewell to Everest

When the Americans came down the mountain they were dirty, unshaved, underweight, and weary. They looked many years older than they were. They didn't smile much. But the human body and mind recover rapidly. After several days of steady marching they began to feel better.

It was a long journey back to Katmandu. Because of Jerstad's frostbitten toes, four Sherpas were assigned to take turns carrying him down the mountain on their backs. It was teamwork with a soul in it. On May 27, they rested at Namche Bazar, where Lute wrote:

Fortunately I am not a serious frostbite case. My fingers and toes are nipped, I might lose a nail or two, but nothing else. I will be okay. Willi and Barry are the ones to worry about. I now ride harnessed on the back of a porter. Four Sherpas take turns carrying me. They are very strong, but not exactly as comfortable as a Greyhound bus! However, it beats hiking on sore toes. With frostbite, the less scuffing and bumping the better the chances of healing. Nevertheless, traveling on a man's back is for the birds. My bones ache and throb. To make matters worse, I don't speak Sherpa and none of my porters can speak a word of English; a great combination for an all-day march. Incidentally, Maynard [Dr. Miller] and Barry [Prather] are still up at Base Camp and will join us later. They've had to do some of their scientific work over again and here's why. Since we first arrived they spent weeks collecting rock and glacier-ice specimens to determine ablation, or surface wasting, and movement of the ice. They hung from wire ladders 80 feet down in crevasses to get snow samples of previous years so that it could be melted down to measure the content of tritium, pollen, dust, salts, and micro-organisms. Later when we came down to Advance Base Camp from our overnight bivouac desperate for something to drink, Maynard gave us his precious samples of water from 20-year-old ice. Now he must risk his life all over again getting more samples from crevasse walls. What a guy!

The monsoon season was threatening the returning expedition. Weather forecasts were unreliable. Sometimes mist hung over the Himalayas like a great coat. Sometimes the rays of the tropical sun turned the skin crab-pink. Sometimes the sun was concealed behind a cloud-streaked sky, and sheet lightning, far off, reddened the cliffs and lower valleys, bringing with it the rumble of thunder many miles away. Sometimes those muffled drums brought torrents of rain, causing the trail to become rivulets of mud. The descent was hard on Lute:

We are camped tonight at a place called Rauje; really it's no place at all. The monsoon rains have started to pelt us now; up high they are freezing cold. This is some night—our bags are wet, and we are wet. We are also very tired, especially my porters. They had to carry me up a steep pass today (to 13,000 feet) and over unbelievably rugged terrain. I wish I could get down and walk like the others, but the doctors warn me not to force my feet.

On Thursday, May 30, Lute wrote of Nima Tensing with gratefulness in his heart:

He has been my Man Friday. He looks after all my personal needs; ties my shoes, changes my socks, gives me things from his own pack to keep me dry. I have never seen such devotion. What friendship! How does one repay the kindness from the depths of another's heart? The look in one's eyes, I guess.

Both the land and the weather were difficult. It rained and it rained. The hills rose to high ridges of almost solid rock in places; the climbers had to go up and over and down, and Lute lived in misery. It was the weather and the terrain and the weather again. If there had been no frostbite to contend with, if Lute had been in perfect health, the downward march would have still been slow and tedious. At Jubing, Lute wrote:

I'm switching to horseback tomorrow. Consideration had been given to flying me out of here, but if I can ride a horse I would like to stay with the guys. It has been tough riding on the backs of porters— and I know the feeling is mutual. They have been miniature Paul Bunyans. The Sherpas will take turns carrying me again if the horse doesn't work out. There's still lots of rocky terrain left over which a horse cannot travel; steep staircases hacked out of cliffs with man-swallowing gorges below. I get enough fright just riding on a man's back without adding the worry of trying to stay astride a clumsy horse.

The diarist's spirits brightened considerably on Sunday, June 2:

My feet are gradually improving. The pain isn't so great now. My hands, though, are still awkward. Will Siri fills my pipe for me, but I can light it myself. We are down out of the snow and cold now, and it sure feels good. We were able to see the valley below us today, cool and green and plush, like paradise. Katmandu is only a week's march from here— it won't be long now.

Phakding. Puiyan. Kharikhola. Jubing. Junbesi. At village after village the streets were lined as they are by Fourth of July parade crowds in the United States, only these crowds were curious and kindly in their receptions as the Americans passed through. The natives were all brightly dressed in traditional attire, and the fact that the returning climbers hadn't shaved for weeks, and were heavy-bearded as well as unbathed, made no difference. At Junbesi, Lute wrote:

Our faith in human nature was reaffirmed at this tiny village today. One of those waiting to greet us upon our arrival was the Sherpa woman whose badly burned body we helicoptered to the hospital at Katmandu in March. She has recovered from the burns and walked up to us with gifts of fresh eggs, milk, meat, and native beer. It was her way of saying thank you for saving her life. . . . I rode a horse today and the traveling was easier. I'll use a horse tomorrow, too. . . . It's raining hard again, making the trail extremely slippery. We must be careful. . . . I got my first haircut in three months tonight. A Sherpa gave it to me. It's great to feel the tingle of air on my head again.

Because of the warming climate, nobody used tents any longer for sleeping. They just threw their blankets and bedrolls down on the ground and slept in the open. Until you sleep under the open skies, you never realize how many shooting stars there are in the heavens. One of the overnight stops was on the edge of a forest of sacred monkeys:

I'm sitting on a log as I write this. Just as I sat down, a party of brown monkeys—*sacred* monkeys with special status—loped across in front of me, swung up into the trees, swaying the branches, and now they are very still, all eyes watching me write. They're the untouchables of the Sherpa world. Every temple has a monkey god. . . . I ran out of horses today and tried walking for a while. The going was slow and painful, but it felt good to get off my rear end for a change. The skin is starting to peel off my fingers now. It looks like jungle rot. Most of the black tips have faded, replacing the dead skin with nice pink flesh. Except for the 25 pounds I have lost, maybe I will look normal once more. Reports by radio from Katmandu indicate that Barry and Willi are suffering complications. Willi has infection, and the doctors are worried. If he doesn't respond to antibiotics it will probably mean amputation. I hear that the National Geographic Society has flown Dr. Eldred D. Mundth, the Navy frostbite specialist, all the way from Bethesda, Maryland, to try and save the toes of Willi and Barry.

A large part of the downward obstacle course was behind the expedition by this time. Katmandu was only a straight march through the lower valley. Though the terrible war against Everest was almost over, Lute's mind was filled with vague regrets. He had a strange feeling of finality about going home. A

201

very vital part of his life was ending. He had had his fill of amazements and more than enough frights to last him a lifetime. To see one avalanche as big as an apartment building, its center resembling the monstrous eye of a tornado, as if a hydrogen explosion had suddenly turned the mountain into a white hell —to see one such snowslide is awe-inspiring, but to skirt the edges of such rolling fury day after day, as the expedition had done, had quite another effect. Lute was indeed looking forward to getting back to civilization.

And so as the Americans clambered down those final miles, soon to disperse and go their separate ways, the feeling of elation-with-despair beat in Lute's chest. On the one hand he was happy to be going home; on the other, he was filled with sadness and regret at the prospect of saying good-by to his companions. There is always a poignancy in parting. During those last three months they had worked as one; had faced the unknown and made it familiar. Modern equipment and scientific instruments had been their weapons, but it was not tools alone that had pushed them to the top; it was the men themselves. The manner in which they had stood up to Everest, the daily risks they faced, fulfilling and even surpassing their leader's confidence in them, was an unmatched experience in human endurance and endeavor. They had been successful beyond their wildest dreams. Consider the records they established: the most men on top of Everest during an ex-

pedition, six (since topped by the 1965 India Everest
Expedition with nine); the most men on top in one
day, four; the first ascent of Everest's West Ridge;
the first traverse—up one side, down another—of
any Himalayan peak; the world's highest overnight
bivouac, 28,200 feet; and many more. For all of these
records, they were leaving behind an imperishable
monument: Jake Breitenbach, the first American to
give his life to Everest.

Native runners had been coming out and meeting the returning expedition almost daily now, bringing huge piles of telegrams and the first congratula-
tory letters. Congratulations from President John F.
Kennedy. Congratulations from other heads of state.
Congratulations from the world's leading Alpine
clubs. The triumphant Americans were astonished
at the reactions all over the world to their success.
"God bless you merry gentlemen," wired one British
matron. Pushing on still with all speed in the heat of
the lower hills, a very weary but happy expedition
arrived at Katmandu in mid-June, several weeks after
leaving Base Camp. So ended one of the great cam-
paigns of mountaineering history. Soon the Americans would be going home to receive the most
longed-for welcome of all: that of their own people
in the United States.

Their task accomplished, the Americans had not
merely climbed Everest; they had felt Everest,
thought Everest, and lived Everest for the 93 cruel

days and nights they were on the mountain. Now that it was all over, what had they learned? Looking back on the long struggle, Barry Bishop, lying in the quiet of the hospital at Katmandu where the doctors were trying desperately to save his frostbitten feet, got to the heart of what it all meant when he said:

"Everest is a harsh and hostile immensity. Whoever challenges it declares war. He must mount his assault with the skill and ruthlessness of a military operation. And when the battle ends, the mountain remains unvanquished. There are no true victors, only survivors."

Postscript

It has been several years now since the American Everest team came down from the Himalayan heights and the curtain closed behind them on one of the most dramatic epics ever staged by man in an assault against nature.

The king had been dethroned. What was left for the climbers? In two words—almost everything.

Lute Jerstad returned to the University of Oregon and taught theater and worked on his Ph.D. in drama; Jim Whittaker went back to Seattle as sales manager of an equipment firm dealing in mountaineering and sports supplies; Barry Bishop was promoted by the National Geographic Society to Secretary of its Committee for Research and Exploration; Dr. Tom Hornbein moved from San Diego to Seattle to join the University of Washington's medical research staff; Dr. Willi Unsoeld rejoined the Peace Corps mission in Nepal; Norman Dyhrenfurth went back to Santa Monica to produce the movie version of the 1963 American Everest Expedition; Dr. Maynard Miller returned to Michigan State University as professor of geology. In short, the various members of the expedition returned to the private worlds from which they had come. For some, however, the road back from Katmandu was long and tedious. . . .

Barry Bishop and Willi Unsoeld were many months in the hospital recuperating from their Everest ordeal. Both suffered severe frostbitten feet and hands—skin that later turned black and sloughed off. At the United Mission Hospital, in Katmandu, doctors willingly worked day and night to save the climbers' feet. All the way from Washington, D.C., came Dr. Melvin M. Payne, Executive Vice-President of the National Geographic Society, bringing Dr. Eldred D. Mundth, Navy frostbite specialist, and the latest drugs. Later, Bishop and Unsoeld were flown back to Washington for more treatments with an experimental drug, but by then it was too late. Gangrene, or tissue death, had set in and both Barry's and Willi's toes had to be amputated. "It isn't so bad, going around without toes," Barry says. "You can adjust to anything when you have to. You simply learn how to walk on your heels, that's all." Bishop also lost parts of the little fingers of each hand.

It is ironic that Unsoeld, who so selflessly spent the night massaging Tom Hornbein's feet to save them from frostbite, should himself be one of those who lost his toes. Hornbein credits Willi for saving his limbs. Both Tom and Jerstad came off the mountain intact.

The body of Jake Breitenbach was never recovered. It still lies somewhere up there in the vast wilderness of rock and ice guarding the summit of the world. The Americans grow philosophical when the death of Jake is mentioned. They know he is buried where he would have wanted to be buried. A Wyoming mountaineer and guide at the time he joined the expedition, the high country was his one main reason for living. He was one of those fellows who is happy only in the mountains.

Since Jake's death, another of the Americans, 31-year-old Dan Doody, has lost his life on a mountain. In the spring of 1965, while scaling icy Mount Washington in New Hampshire, the rangy climber-photographer had reached an elevation of 5,100 feet when he slipped and fell about 1,000 feet. He was killed instantly. "In mountain climbing," Dan had said shortly before plunging to his death, "when you lose, there is no next time."

In the two years since Jerstad returned from Everest he has had ample time to think about that terrible night he and his three companions bivouaced at 28,200 feet, and put it in its proper perspective. "It was a strange night in many ways," he reflects. "We had estimated that going without oxygen for three or four hours at that elevation would lead to death or irreparable brain damage. By all standards we had no business coming out of it alive. But we did. Despite the odds we *knew* we'd get through the night. Maybe all men feel as confident in the face of death. I don't know. I can only speak for myself. I've been in many situations when all hope vanished and death seemed certain, yet here I am. You may say that our Everest experiences are proof positive that God does exist; that we came down off that mountain alive because the killing wind mysteriously *stopped blowing* on the only night we were trapped high up and couldn't get down. To the believers, it proves there is a Divine Being and He was watching over us; to others, it may only be a coincidence. A fantastic miracle. If I had to climb Everest to find God, then I am fooling myself."

On the morning of July 8, 1963, American mountaineering received its highest accolade. In the Rose Garden of the White House, President John F. Kennedy shook hands with each member of the American Everest Expedition and formally presented the team with the National Geographic Society's gold Hubbard Medal—the highest honor Americans of adventure can receive.

"In giving this medal to the expedition," said the President, "I carry on a great tradition, as do they in demonstrating that the vigorous life still attracts Americans."

In accepting the Hubbard Medal on behalf of the American team, Norman Dyhrenfurth replied, "I believe this is the first time American mountaineers have been so honored. In other words, American mountaineering has come of age." He then gave the President an American flag that had been carried to Everest's summit by Barry Bishop and Lute Jerstad.

That Americans climbed Everest is not the most important point we have attempted to make in this book. That they *wanted* to climb Everest in the first place means everything. "It is the ultimate wisdom of the mountains that a man is never more a man than when he is striving for what is beyond his grasp," says James Ramsey Ullman, "and that there is no conquest worth the winning save that over his own weakness and ignorance and fear." It was not the summit that mattered, but the struggle along the way; not the final triumph, but the adventure itself.

Mount Everest has been won, but so, too, have the poles been reached, the oceans spanned, the jungles threaded—and space explored. That does not necessarily mean that for the Americans who climbed Everest their dreams are finished or that they have packed away their climbing axes and ropes for the last time. There will always be other challenges to face. Other trials and triumphs are still ahead for those who are willing to try. The vanquished peak of the earth's tallest mountain certainly does not end it for Jerstad. "Everest doesn't interest me any more," says Lute. "I've already been there. It's done. But there are other mountains and other challenges—and I'll be there." His fellow members of the Everest Expedition feel much the same, for life goes on for them, and, like other mortals, they are built to look forward, not back. As one era closes for them, new ones loom invitingly just beyond the next horizon.

Now the curtain closes on our story. The sun goes down. The great peaks sleep the night away. But there will be more tomorrows. And more young Americans forever ready to accept the challenge of the unknown.

Appendix

211

Kharikhola (kâ·rēk·hō′lâ)
Khimti Khola (river) (kēm′tē kō′lâ)
Khumbu Glacier (kūm′bū)
Khumbu Icefall
Khumjung (kūm′jŭng)
Lho La Pass (hlō lâ)
Lhotse (hlô′tse)
the Lhotse Face
Likhu Khola (river) (lē′kū kō′lâ)
Lobujya (lō·būj′yâ)
Makalu (mŭ′kâ·lū)
Mount Everest (ev′ə·rəst)
Namche Bazar (nâm′chē bə·zâr′)
Nuptse (nūp′tse)
Panch-khal (pânch′kôl)
Pangboche (pâng·bō′che)
Phakding (p'hâk′dĭng)
Pheriche (p'he′rē·che)
Puiyan (pwē′yân)
Pumori (pū·mô′rē)
Rauje (rou′je) 202
Risingo (rĭ·sĭng′gō)
Sete (se′tē)
Sola Khola Valley (sō′lâ kō′lâ)
the South Col
Taksindhu (tâk·sĭn·dū′)
Taksindhu Col
Those (tō′sē)
Thyangboche (tyâng·bō′che)
the West Shoulder
the Yellow Band
Yersa (yer′sâ)

212

*Glossary of Mountaineering Terms with
Pronunciations*

Alp: a mountain pasture.

Belay: securing a rope by hitching it over a projection or passing it around the body.

Bivouac (bē·vwak′) : a temporary camp.

Chimney: a steep, narrow cleft in a rock wall.

Col (kôl) : a pass, or the low point of a ridge.

Corniche (kôr·nēsh′) : a projecting mass of snow, as on a ridge.

Couloir (kū·lwar′) : a gully.

Crampons (krā·põ′) : iron or steel frames, with projecting spikes, that are attached to the soles of the boots for use on steep snow or ice.

Crevasse (krə·vas′) : a deep crack in a glacier, caused by its downward movement.

Cwm (kūm) : a hollow in a mountainside; a deep ravine.

Glissade (glē·sad′) : sliding down a snow slope.

Icefall: the steepest section of a glacier, usually taking the form of a wildly jumbled mass of ice.

Pitch: a short, steep section of rock.

Piton (pē·tõ′) : a metal spike which may be driven into rock or ice to afford support for hand, foot, or rope.

Rappel (ra·pel′) : roping down. The maneuver of letting oneself down a steep place by means of supplementary rope.

Sherpas (sher′pəs) : hillmen of Tibetan stock from eastern Nepal.

Traverse (tra·vers′) : the horizontal or diagonal crossing of a mountainside; also the crossing of a peak or pass from one side to the other.

DATE DUE

MAR 31			
APR 14			
MAY 3			
OCT 2			
OCT 24			
DEC 19			
OCT 14			
JAN 28			
JAN 27			
JAN 27			
GAYLORD			PRINTED IN U.S.A.